INDEX TO OBITUARY NOTICES
in the
Richmond Enquirer from May 9, 1804,
through 1828,
and the
Richmond Whig from January, 1824,
through 1838.

Edited by
H. R. McIlwaine

CLEARFIELD

Originally published as
Bulletin of the Virginia State Library
Vol. XIV, No. 4, October, 1921
Richmond, Virginia, 1923

Reprinted by
Genealogical Publishing Co., Inc.
Baltimore, Maryland
1974, 1979

Library of Congress Catalogue Card Number 74-15235

Reprinted for Clearfield Company by
Genealogical Publishing Company
Baltimore, Maryland
1994, 1996, 2010

ISBN 978-0-8063-0633-9

Made in the United States of America

PREFACE

This index was originally prepared by several members of the apprentice class of the Virginia State Library in 1904, under the direction of Mr. John P. Kennedy, at that time librarian. It was probably Mr. Kennedy's intention to have cards written for both the *Enquirer* and the *Whig* for the entire period of their existence, and to print the work as part of one of the annual reports of the library, but he left the service of the library before this could be done—only a small part of this work, in fact, as originally designed, having been completed. Of the *Enquirer* only the years 1804-1828 had been gone over, and of the *Whig* only the years 1824-1838. Neither set of cards had been revised. Even in this condition, however, the cards have frequently been consulted here at the State Library by genealogical and historical workers. It has been for some years the hope of the present librarian to finish the work and have it printed as one of the numbers of the Library Bulletin. But it has not been possible to do this. The number of workers on the library staff has never been sufficient. The cards have now been revised, however, and arranged in one alphabet, and the time appears to be so remote when the whole work can be done that it has been determined to print the cards as they are without further delay.

The persons referred to in the obituary notices were probably, in ninety-nine cases out of a hundred, residents of Virginia, and usually natives, but occasionally the reference is to a former Virginian who had removed from the State, or to some person having no special connection with the State, but whose death for some reason or other was taken note of in the "obituary column." The index does not cover the news columns, wherein are to be found items in reference to the death of persons of nation-wide interest. The special aim has been to include only Virginians.

The entries have been made as brief as possible. First comes the name, then the part of the State of which the person was a resident, if given, then the paper (the *Enquirer* or the *Whig*), the date of the paper, and the number of the page. Very rarely an obituary notice of a person appears in each of the papers. Occasionally the name of the person's home is given, sometimes with, and sometimes without, the name of the county. Once in a while in the obituary notice the residence of the subject of the notice is not given. Probably in the great majority of such cases this residence was Richmond. The omission has in no case been supplied, however, but has been indicated by a line, ——————.

The file of neither paper possessed by the library is absolutely complete, there being issues missing here and there, and these gaps explain the occasional omissions from the list of notices of well known persons. Our files are about as nearly complete, however, as files of papers of the period covered usually are, and it was not practicable to have the files in the Library of Congress and in other large depositories examined for supplemental numbers. This publication, accordingly, has many deficiencies, but the use of the great number of cards written will be so much extended by printing, that it is thought the cost will be justified.

The name of the *Whig* at the start was the *Constitutional Whig*. It was published as a semi-weekly under this name till 1833. In the meanwhile the *Richmond Daily Whig* made its appearance, in November, 1828, and was published for several years concurrently with the *Constitutional Whig*, and under the same general management, John Hampden Pleasants being editor of each. In 1833 the *Constitutional Whig* became the *Richmond Whig and Public Advertiser*, retaining this title and being published as a semi-weekly, through the period for which these cards were written. In the index, however, in order to save space, merely the form *Whig* is used for the publication appearing under these several names.

With this number of the Bulletin of the Virginia State Library, its appearance as a quarterly publication will be discontinued. There is sufficient material collected and now in final form to bring the publication of the Bulletin up to date, but funds are lacking. There is now being published by the library the Minutes of the General Court of Colonial Virginia, the cost of which will more than absorb the balance to the credit of the amount appropriated by the General Assembly of Virginia, at the 1922 session, for State Library publications, and no more funds will be available till March 1, 1924, nearly a year hence, after the passage of the next appropriation act. It seems best, accordingly, to continue the Bulletin in the future, not as a quarterly, but merely as an occasional publication, the numbers of which will appear as funds and material may be available. The next number to be expected, then, will be No. 1 of Vol. XV, but it will be given the date of actual publication, and not the date of January, 1922, which would be necessitated by adherence to the "quarterly" convention.

H. R. McILWAINE.

A

Abbott, Mrs. Eliza, Hanover, Enquirer, Feb. 14, 1822, 3
Abbott, Mrs. Virginia, Richmond, Whig, Nov. 9, 1830, 3
Abbott, Wm. D., ——————, Enquirer, April 12, 1825, 3
Abrahams, Mrs. Mary, Richmond, Whig, Aug. 11, 1837, 1
Abrams, Judge Henry, Ohio [formerly of Virginia], Enquirer, Dec. 15, 1821, 3
Adams, Mrs. Apphia, Williamsburg, Whig, June 21, 1830, 3
Adams, Elizabeth G., Richmond, Whig, Nov. 16, 1832, 3
Adams, Dr. John, Richmond, Enquirer, June 28, 1825, 3; Whig, June 24, 1825, 3.
Adams, Palmer, Lynchburg, Enquirer, Sept. 4, 1821, 3
Adams, Mrs. Richard, ——————, Enquirer, October 20, 1809, 3
Adams, Samuel, Virginia, Enquirer, Aug. 30, 1815, 3
Adams, Samuel G., Richmond, Enquirer, July 17, 1821, 3
Adams, Mrs. Sarah, Richmond, Enquirer, June 10, 1815, 3
Adams, Miss Tabitha, Richmond, Enquirer, Feb. 19, 1828, 3; Whig, Feb. 13, 1828, 3
Adcock, William, Buckingham, Enquirer, Oct. 9, 1827, 3
Adcock, Capt. William, Henrico, Whig, March 17, 1834, 3
Adie, Benjamin, Prince William, Enquirer, Nov. 4, 1823, 3
Adie, Mrs. Eleanor, Richmond, Whig, Jan. 2, 1835, 1
Adkins, Thomas, Richmond, Whig, Oct. 19, 1830, 3
Albers, Dr. J. A., Richmond, Enquirer, May 22, 1821, 4
Alexander, Charles Eaton, Mecklenburg, Enquirer, Oct. 26, 1827, 3
Alexander, Mrs. Fanny A., Charlotte, Whig, May 13, 1834, 4
Alexander, Col. Mark, Mecklenburg, Enquirer, Aug. 10, 1824, 3
Alexander, Mrs. Sarah, King William, Whig, June 23, 1837, 2
Allen, Frances, Richmond, Whig, Aug. 6, 1829, 3
Allen, Mrs. Frances R., Richmond, Whig, Feb. 30, 1829, 2
Allen, James C., Richmond, Whig, Aug. 3, 1838, 2
Allen, Mary Ann, Richmond, Whig, June 13, 1834, 2
Allen, Robert W., Caroline, Whig, March 26, 1836, 1
Allen, Thomas Diddep, Richmond, Whig, Jan. 12, 1832, 3
Allen, Lieut. Com'dt. Wm. H., Enquirer, Dec. 3, 1822, 2, 3; Dec. 5, 1822, 1; Dec. 10, 1822, 2
Allen, William, Buckingham, Enquirer, March 16, 1824, 3
Allen, William L., James City, Enquirer, Oct. 21, 1823, 3
Allmand, Col. Albert, Richmond, Whig, April 25, 1831, 3
Allman, ——————, Norfolk, Enquirer, April 13, 1821, 4
Alsop, Benjamin, Jr., Spottsylvania, Whig, July, 30, 1833, 3
Alston, Willis, Richmond, Enquirer, Sept. 14, 1827, 3
Ambler, Mrs., Richmond, Enquirer, Aug. 5, 1806, 3
Ambler, Augusta, Rappahannock, Whig, July 18, 1837, 2
Ambler, Col. John, Richmond, Whig, April 12, 1836, 3
Ambler, John P., Rappahannock, Whig, July 21, 1837, 2
Ames, Benjamin, Richmond, Enquirer, Oct. 27, 1812, 3

Ames, Mrs. Hannah, Goochland, Enquirer, Sept. 15, 1818, 3
Ames, Julia Ann, Goochland, Enquirer, Sept. 15, 1818, 3
Anderson, Agnes, Nelson, Whig, July 20, 1838, 4
Anderson, Alexander, Hanover, Enquirer, Jan. 17, 1822, 3
Anderson, Col. Andrew, Augusta, Enquirer, June 24, 1823, 3
Anderson, Bartlett, Hanover, Enquirer, May 9, 1823, 3
Anderson, Chas. B., Prince Edward, Whig, July 30, 1833, 1
Anderson, Cuthbert Steel, Logan, Enquirer, Nov. 4, 1823, 3
Anderson, Daniel L., Prince Edward, Enquirer, Oct. 14, 1828, 3
Anderson, David, Richmond, Whig, March 20, 1835, 2
Anderson, Izates, Cherry Point, Enquirer, Sept. 16, 1823, 3
Anderson, James, New Kent, Enquirer, May 7, 1813, 3
Anderson, John, Montgomery C. H., Enquirer, March 27, 1821, 3
Anderson, John T., Cumberland, Enquirer, Nov. 20, 1821, 3
Anderson, Joseph, Richmond, Whig, April 21, 1837, 1
Anderson, Leroy, Williamsburg, Whig, Dec. 1, 1837, 2
Anderson, Mandaville R., Albemarle, Whig, Jan. 5, 1838, 1
Anderson, Mrs. Marcia, Louisa, Enquirer, July 3, 1821, 3
Anderson, Mrs. Margaret L., Richmond, Whig, May 21, 1833, 2
Anderson, Mrs. Maria, Richmond, Whig, July 11, 1826, 3; Enquirer, July 11, 1826, 3
Anderson, Mrs. Martha M., Nottoway, Whig, July 14, 1837, 4
Anderson, Nathaniel, Albemarle, Enquirer, Feb. 8, 1812, 3
Anderson, Overton, Richmond, Enquirer, Dec. 12, 1809, 3
Anderson, Col. Patrick, Hanover, Whig, Aug. 31, 1824, 3; Enquirer, Sept. 24, 1824, 3
Anderson, Rev. Peyton, Culpeper C. H., Enquirer, Sept. 9, 1823, 3
Anderson, Richard H., Richmond, Whig, Jan. 17, 1831, 3
Anderson, Richard Louthur, Richmond, Whig, June 7, 1833, 1
Anderson, Capt. Robert, Williamsburg, Enquirer, June 29, 1813, 3
Anderson, Samuel, Cumberland, Enquirer, May 2, 1826, 3
Anderson, Mrs. Susan, Richmond, Whig, July 11, 1826, 3; Enquirer, July 11, 1826, 3
Anderson, Wm. M., Halifax, Enquirer, June 24, 1828, 3
Andrew, Mrs. Catharine Urbania, Richmond, Whig, July 19, 1828, 3
Andrew, Rev. John F., Richmond, Whig, Jan. 7, 1830, 3
Andrew, Robert, Richmond, Whig, Oct. 27, 1831, 4
Andrew, Samuel, Richmond, Whig, Oct. 31, 1834, 1
Andrews, John, Williamsburg, Whig, Oct. 10, 1834, 3
Andrews, Mrs. Mary Blair, Williamsburg, Enquirer, Jan. 20, 1820, 3
Anglea, Mrs. Sarah, Cumberland, Whig, March 12, 1836, 1
Anthony, Christopher, Lynchburg, Whig, Oct. 13, 1835, 1; Oct. 16, 1835, 3
Anthony, John, Hanover, Enquirer, Feb. 13, 1817, 3
Apperson, Jane Elenor, Mecklenburg, Enquirer, Aug. 16, 1825, 3
Archer, Mrs. Anna Eliza, Powhatan, Enquirer, Oct. 27, 1826, 3
Archer, Charlotte, Powhatan, Enquirer, Oct. 27, 1826, 3
Archer, John, Amelia, Enquirer, March 24, 1812, 3
Archer, Logan, Powhatan, Enquirer, Oct. 27, 1826, 3
Archer, Maj. Peter F., Powhatan, Enquirer, May 25, 1814, 3

Archer, Richard C., Norfolk, Whig, July 2, 1824, 3
Archer, Dr. Robert P., Chesterfield, Whig, Aug. 16, 1829, 3
Archer, William, Powhatan, Enquirer, Oct. 11, 1822, 3
Archer, Wm. Abner, Powhatan, Whig, Oct. 21, 1836, 2
Armistead, Capt. Addison Bowles, Fort Moultrie, Enquirer, March 16, 1813, 3
Armistead, Mrs. Frances, Cumberland, Whig, Jan. 28, 1832, 1
Armistead, Rev. J. S., Buckingham, Whig, July 6, 1832, 3
Armistead, James A., Cartersville, Enquirer, June 5, 1827, 3
Armistead, John, Enquirer, Feb. 17, 1825, 1
Armistead, John M., Norfolk, Whig, Dec. 30, 1831, 1
Armistead, Mrs. Mary, Portsmouth, Whig, Nov. 21, 1828, 3
Armistead, Theodorick, Norfolk, Enquirer, Dec. 3, 1812, 3
Armistead, Major W., ————, Enquirer, Oct. 3, 1809, 3
Armistead, Wm., King and Queen, Whig, Feb. 6, 1827, 3
Armstrong, Amzi Stockton, Richmond, Whig, Aug. 3, 1832, 3
Arnold, Thomas, Petersburg, Enquirer, Oct. 4, 1822, 3
Asbury, Francis, ————, Enquirer, April 10, 1816, 3
Ashlin, John, Fluvanna, Enquirer, Feb. 13, 1823, 3; Feb. 18, 1823, 3
Ast, William F., Richmond, Enquirer, Sept. 26, 1807, 3
Aston, John, Powhatan, Whig, April 18, 1837, 2
Atherton, Mrs. Phebe, Richmond, Enquirer, Oct. 14, 1806, 3
Atkinson, Mrs. Agnes, Chesterfield, Enquirer, Dec. 11, 1821, 3
Atkinson, Lewis, ————, Enquirer, Dec. 1, 1814, 3
Atkinson, Mrs. Mary T., Dinwiddie, Enquirer, March 25, 1823, 3
Atkinson, Robert, Mansfield, Enquirer, May 18, 1821, 3
Austin, Dr. Archibald, Bedford, Enquirer, Oct. 11, 1814, 4
Austin, Mrs. Catherine, Richmond, Whig, Oct. 9, 1832, 1
Austin, John, Sr., Hanover, Enquirer, Dec. 19, 1815, 3
Austin, Mrs. Melissa M., Cumberland, Whig, Aug. 15, 1834, 1
Austin, Major William, Richmond, Enquirer, May 1, 1807, 3
Avis, Rev. James, Jefferson, Enquirer, Nov. 23, 1824, 3
Aylett, Mrs. Elizabeth H., King William, Enquirer, Nov. 27, 1818, 3
Aylett, Louisa, King William, Enquirer, Sept. 6, 1822, 3
Ayres, Nathan, Buckingham, Enquirer, Jan. 26, 1822, 3

B.

Baber, Mrs. Emily, King George, Whig, July 10, 1835, 3
Baber, Harden, [formerly of Richmond], Whig, Sept. 13, 1833, 1
Bacchus, Gurdon, ————, Enquirer, Dec. 22, 1810, 3
Bacchus, Gurdon H., Richmond, Whig, Dec. 12, 1834, 4
Backhouse, Mrs. Judith D., Gloucester, Whig, March 21, 1834, 4
Bacon, Elizabeth, Louisa, Whig, June 29, 1838, 1
Bacon, Izard, Henrico, Enquirer, Jan. 11, 1816, 3
Bagby, Mrs. Elizabeth, King and Queen, Whig, Oct. 11, 1836, 1
Bagby, James, Powhatan, Whig, June 15, 1824, 3
Bailey, Caroline M., Richmond, Whig, Sept. 21, 1832, 1
Bailey, Capt. James, Surry, Whig, June 24, 1836, 3

Bailey, Joen Lewis, Fredericksburg, Whig, March 1, 1832, 3
Bailey, Joseph, Henrico, Whig, Oct. 27, 1831, 4,
Bailey, Mrs. Nancy, Richmond, Whig, July 30, 1830, 3
Bailey, Capt. Wm., Surry, Whig, Sept. 17, 1828, 3
Baker, Jerman, Richmond, Whig, March 29, 1828, 3
Baker, Julia Clementine, Orange, Whig, Oct. 13, 1835, 3
Baldwin, Dr. Cornelius, Winchester, Enquirer, Jan. 2, 1827, 3
Baldwin, George, Amelia, Enquirer, Feb. 13, 1817, 3
Baldwin, Dr. Wm. D., Winchester, Whig, March 8, 1830, 3
Ball, Mrs. Elizabeth, Richmond, Whig, July 29, 1829, 3
Ball, George, Gloucester, Enquirer, Nov. 20, 1812, 3
Ball, Col. James, Lancaster, Enquirer, March 9, 1826, 3
Ball, Margaret J., Hanover, Whig, Sept. 26, 1837, 2
Ball, William, Winchester, Enquirer, May 29, 1813, 2
Ball, William Lee, Richmond, Enquirer, March 4, 1824, 2 & 3; April 2, 1824, 3
Ballard, Elisha, Isle of Wight, Whig, Dec. 8, 1835, 3
Ballard, Mrs. Elizabeth, [formerly of Richmond], Enquirer, Nov. 14, 1823, 3
Bankhead, Mrs. Anne, Charlottesville, Enquirer, Feb. 23, 1826, 3
Bankhead, Stewart, Westmoreland, Enquirer, May 14, 1805, 3
Bankley, John, Warm Springs, Enquirer, Dec. 11, 1827, 3
Banks, Alexander, Manchester, Enquirer, Dec. 1, 1807, 3
Banks, Mrs. Catharine, Essex, Enquirer, Nov. 8, 1814, 3
Banks, Eliza, Tappahannock, Enquirer, Oct. 28, 1814, 3
Banks, Maj. George Washington, Yorktown, Whig, Oct. 2, 1835, 1
Banks, John, Richmond, Enquirer, Oct. 20, 1809, 3
Banks, Mrs. Margaret Wilson, Richmond, Whig, July 17, 1832, 3
Banks, Mrs. Martha Koyall [Royall], Richmond, Enquirer, Dec. 6, 1804, 3
Banks, Col. Tunstall, Yorktown, Enquirer, Feb. 20, 1827, 3
Barbour, Benj. Johnson, Orange, Enquirer, July 11, 1820, 3
Barbour, Mrs. Mary, Barboursville, Enquirer, Aug. 13, 1826, 3; Aug. 18, 1826, 3
Barbour, Col. Thomas, Barboursville, Enquirer, May 24, 1825, 3
Barker, Elizabeth B., Richmond, Whig, May 15, 1838, 2
Barksdale, Rev. John, Charlottesville, Whig, Oct. 5, 1829, 3
Barksdale, Wm., Richmond, Whig, Oct. 15, 1824, 3
Barksdale, Wm., ——————, Enquirer, Oct. 7, 1828, 3
Barnes, Richard, Tappahannock, Enquirer, June 20, 1820, 3
Barns, Major Luther, Richmond, Whig, June 21, 1830, 3
Barr, Philip, Near Richmond, Whig, Aug. 28, 1829, 3
Barraud, Dr. John T., Norfolk, Enquirer, June 12, 1821, 3
Barraud, Dr. Philip, Nansemond, Whig, Dec. 6, 1830, 3
Barreb, Mrs. Caroline, Williamsburg, Enquirer, April 12, 1811, 3
Barrett, Mrs. Catherine, Manchester, Whig, Aug. 27, 1833, 2
Barrett, Mrs. Sarah G., Amelia, Enquirer, Oct. 11, 1825, 3
Barrett, William F., Fluvanna, Enquirer, April 3, 1823, 3; April 8, 1823, 3
Barrom, Mrs. Elizabeth, Norfolk, Enquirer, July 8, 1823, 3
Barron, Commodore Samuel, Norfolk, Enquirer, Nov. 6, 1810, 3

Barrow, Wm. E., Richmond, Whig, Sept. 16, 1836, 3
Barton, Mrs. Alcinda W., Culpeper, Whig, Jan. 5, 1830, 3
Bass, Edward, Sr., Chesterfield, Whig, May 27, 1834, 4.
Bass, Richard W., Powhatan, Whig, Aug. 28, 1838, 2
Bates, Benjamin, Hanover, Enquirer, Dec. 19, 1812, 3
Bates, Fleming, Northumberland, Whig, Jan. 8, 1831, 3; Feb. 9, 1831, 3
Bates, William, Jefferson, Enquirer, Sept. 20, 1822, 3
Battaile, Mrs. Frances C., Caroline, Enquirer, Aug. 12, 1828, 3
Baugh, Archibald, Petersburg, Enquirer, April 9, 1824, 3
Baugh, Mrs. Sarah, Manchester, Whig, Feb. 23, 1833, 3
Baxter, George C., Lexington, Whig, Nov. 27, 1835, 2
Baylor, Mrs. Lucy, Shepherdstown, Whig, Jan. 15, 1836, 4
Baylor, Thomas L., King and Queen, Enquirer, Sept. 3, 1822, 3
Bayly, Wm. P., Stafford, Whig, Dec. 20, 1836, 4
Baynham, Mrs. Joanna, —————, Enquirer, Dec. 15, 1807, 3
Baytop, Major James, Hampton, Enquirer, Jan. 2, 1821, 3
Beale, Col. John, —————, Enquirer, Oct. 31, 1809, 3
Beall, Mrs. William D., Jefferson, Whig, Feb. 10, 1837, 2
Beard, Mrs. Sarah, Louisa, Enquirer, Jan. 31, 1826, 3
Beasley, Maj., Prince Edward, Enquirer, Oct. 12, 1813, 4
Beasley, Joseph, Richmond, Enquirer, May 26, 1812, 3
Beck, John Augustus, Richmond, Whig, Sept. 13, 1833, 1
Belcher, John, Chesterfield, Whig, Dec. 23, 1824, 3; Dec. 28, 1824, 3
Bell, Alexander, Richmond, Enquirer, Dec. 24, 1812, 3
Bell, Caroline, Petersburg, Enquirer, June 16, 1826, 3
Bell, John, Richmond, Enquirer, Aug. 10, 1821, 3
Bell, Capt. John Haywood, Westmoreland, Whig, Aug. 23, 1833, 1
Bell, Mrs. Mary, Petersburg, Enquirer, June 16, 1826, 3
Bell, Peyton, Richmond and Petersburg, Whig, June 13, 1834, 2
Bell, Robert, Richmond, Enquirer, Aug. 14, 1827, 3; Whig, Aug. 11, 1827, 3
Bell, Mrs. Sarah, Hanover, Enquirer, Oct. 19, 1819, 3
Bell, Mrs. Susan D., Henrico, Whig, Jan. 7, 1835, 3
Bell, Capt. Wm., Henrico, Enquirer, Oct. 11, 1825, 3
Bellamy, Mrs. Martha, Richmond, Enquirer, Feb. 24, 1821, 3
Belt, Dr. John Singleton, Cumberland, Enquirer, Sept. 21, 1827, 3
Bendle, Reuben, Richmond, Whig, July 27, 1832, 3
Bendle, Thomas, Richmond, Whig, Feb. 25, 1825, 3
Bennett, Rebecca S., Richmond, Whig, Dec. 30, 1830, 3
Benson, Miss, Fredericksburg, Enquirer, Oct. 4, 1822, 3
Bentley, Efford, —————, Whig, Aug. 1, 1837, 2
Berg, Mrs. Osborne, Goochland, Whig, July 17, 1832, 1
Berkeley, Lewis, Richmond, Whig, May 17, 1836, 1
Berkley, Capt. Edmund, Hanover, Enquirer, April 21, 1820, 3
Berkley, Mrs. Landon, Hanover, Enquirer, June 21, 31, 1815, 3
Berkley, Nelson, Prince Edward, Enquirer, Dec. 19, 1826, 3
Berkley, Thomas Nelson, Hanover, Enquirer, Sept. 26, 1823, 3
Berkley, Wm. Randolph, Prince Edward, Whig, Oct. 29, 1833, 1
Bernard, Mrs. Elizabeth, Albemarle, Enquirer, Sept. 10, 1822, 3

Bernard, Jesse, —————, Enquirer, Jan. 3, 1828, 3
Bernard, William, Port Royal, Enquirer, Feb. 9, 1822, 3
Berteau, Armistead, Richmond, Whig, Sept. 20, 1833, 1
Betts, Lieut. Chas., Northumberland, Enquirer, Jan. 22, 1822, 3
Beveley, George, Campbell, Enquirer, Dec. 31, 1822, 3
Beveley, Harriot, Campbell, Enquirer, Dec. 17, 1822, 3
Beveley, Jane, Essex, Enquirer, Oct. 18, 1822, 3
Beveley, Rebecca Tayloe, Essex, Enquirer, Oct. 11, 18, 1822, 3
Bibb, Lucien F., Bellona Arsenal, Whig, Sept. 12, 1831, 3
Biggart, Robert, Warwick, Whig, Oct. 4, 1836, 4
Biggers, Adolphus E. L., Richmond, Whig, Jan. 29, 1829, 3
Biggs, Brig. Gen. Benjamin, —————, Enquirer, Dec. 30, 1823, 3
Binford, Frances Ann T., Henrico, Whig, April 18, 1830, 3
Binford, Henry E., Richmond, Whig, Dec. 1, 1835, 1
Bingham, Isaac, Richmond [formerly of Connecticut], Enquirer, July 17, 1816, 3
Bingham, Robert, Gosport, Whig, Dec. 25, 1829, 3
Bingham, Samuel, Richmond, Whig, Oct. 23, 1835, 2
Biscoe, Henry L., Manchaster, Enquirer, July 24, 1810, 3
Bishop, Mrs. Ann, —————, Enquirer, Jan. 3, 1805, 3
Blackburn, George, Columbia, S. C., Enquirer, Aug. 29, 1823, 3
Blackburn, Martha E., Henrico, Whig, Oct. 26, 1829, 3
Blackburn, Gen. Samuel, Bath, Whig, March 10, 1835, 1
Blackburn, Mrs. Sarah, Middlesex, Enquirer, Oct. 2, 1827, 3
Blackford, Mrs. Benj., Page, Whig, Feb. 3, 1837, 1
Blackwell, David, Hanover, Whig, Jan. 9, 1838, 4
Blackwell, Col. Hiram, Northumberland, Enquirer, Feb. 1, 1823, 3
Blackwell, Gen. John, Fauquier, Enquirer, June 20, 1823, 3
Blackwell, Major Joseph, Fauquier, Whig, Nov. 3, 1826, 3
Blackwell, Col. Samuel, Northumberland, Whig, June 6, 1837, 4
Blackwell, Thomas, Richmond, Enquirer, May 18, 1819, 3
Blackwood, Mrs Elizabeth, Richmond, Whig, Jan. 5, 1835, 3
Blagrove, Charles, Richmond, Enquirer, Aug. 20, 1814, 3
Blair, Archibald, Richmond, Enquirer, Oct. 8, 1824, 3
Blair, Eldest son of Mr. Archibald Blair, Richmond, Enquirer, Nov. 20, 1827, 3
Blair, Dr. James, Richmond, Whig, Oct. 6, 1835, 2
Blair, Rev. John D., Richmond, Enquirer, Jan. 11, 1823, 3; Jan. 14, 1823, 3
Blair, John H., Hanover, Whig, Nov. 21, 1827, 3; Enquirer, Nov. 20, 1827, 3
Blair, Mrs. Mary, Richmond, Whig, Oct. 6, 1831, 3
Blair, Walter, Richmond, Whig, Aug. 9, 1830, 2
Blake, Jacob, Matthews, Enquirer, Feb. 16, 1819, 3
Blakey, Reuben S., Henrico, Whig, Aug. 20, 1833, 4
Blakey, George, Henrico, Whig, Dec. 17, 1824, 3
Blakey, Thomas, Newcastle, Enquirer, Dec. 31, 1805, 3
Blamire, John H., Norfolk, Whig, April 29, 1831, 3
Block, Mrs. Mary, Albemarle, Enquirer, May 25, 1819, 3
Block, William, Rocketts, Whig, Aug. 16, 1825, 3

Blondel, John M., Caroline, Whig, July 27, 1838, 2
Blount, Benjamin, Southampton, Enquirer, Feb. 14, 1826, 3
Blount, Mrs. Francis, Powhatan, Enquirer, March 12, 1822, 3
Blount, Thompson, Powhatan, Enquirer, May 9, 1828, 3
Blunt, James, Caroline, Whig, Jan. 26, 1832, 3
Bockieus, Mrs. B. C., Malvern Hill, Whig, Jan. 13, 1826, 3
Bockins, Mrs. Betty Carter, Henrico, Enquirer, Jan. 12, 1826, 3
Bockius, Jacob, Richmond, Enquirer, June 2, 1804, 3
Bockius, Mrs. Mary Ann R., Malvern Hill, Whig, April 8, 11, 1834, 1
Bohannon, Alexander S., Richmond, Whig, May 18, 1829, 3
Boisseau, Daniel, Chesterfield, Enquirer, Feb. 5, 1824, 3
Bolding, Jane Rolfe, Richmond, Whig, Aug. 29, 1831, 3
Bolling, Archibald, Campbell, Enquirer, Sept. 4, 1827, 3
Bolling, Lenaeus, Buckingham, Whig, Jan. 28, 1836, 3; Feb. 23, 1836, 3
Bolling, Linnaeus, Buckingham, Enquirer, June 5, 1816, 3
Bolling, Martha Storrs, Powhatan, Whig, Sept. 8, 1837, 4
Bolling, Mrs. Mary, Buckingham, Whig, Jan. 28, 1825, 3; Enquirer, Jan.
    27, 1825, 3
Bolling, Pocahontas Ann, Richmond, Whig, May 31, 1836, 1
Bolling, Pocahontas A., [formerly of Richmond], Whig, April 3, 1838, 4
Bondurant, Sarah Eliza, Buckingham, Whig, Dec. 29, 1837, 2
Booker, Alfred, Richmond, Enquirer, Oct. 12, 1816, 3
Booker, Arthur G., Amelia, Enquirer, Jan. 9, 1821, 3
Booker, John, Amherst, Enquirer, Aug. 6, 1805, 3
Booker, Lewis, Essex, Whig, March 13, 1832, 3
Booker, Capt. Lewis, Essex, Enquirer, Jan. 11, 1815, 3
Booker, Pinkethmam D., Amelia, Enquirer, Oct. 10, 1825, 3
Booker, Mary Jane, Prince Edward, Whig, May 8, 1835, 3
Booker, Richard, Cumberland, Enquirer, May 1, 1818, 3
Booker, William, Amelia, Enquirer, Jan. 23, 1821, 3
Booth, George Wythe, Gloucester, Enquirer, Jan. 7, 1809, 3
Booth, Mary E., Goochland, Enquirer, Sept. 18, 1818, 3
Booth, Dr. Robert N., Dinwiddie, Whig, Aug. 28, 1838, 4
Bootwright, Mrs. Sarah, Richmond, Whig, April 15, 1831, 3
Bosher, John, Richmond, Whig, Sept. 28, 1832, 1
Bosher, Mrs. Maria, Richmond, Enquirer, March 22, 1815, 3
Boswell, Dr. Thomas, Gloucester, Whig, Sept. 13, 1833, 1
Bott, Miles, near Manchester, Whig, Oct. 23, 1835, 4,
Bottom, Theophilus J., Amelia, Whig, Dec. 29, 1835, 3
Botts, Benjamin, Richmond, Enquirer, Jan. 4, 7, 1812, 3
Bouldin, Mrs. Ann B., Charlotte, Enquirer, Jan. 6, 8, 1824, 3
Bouldin, Mrs. Martha, Mecklenburg, Enquirer, July 24, 1827, 3
Bouldin, Hon. Thomas T., Campbell, Whig, March 21, 1834, 1
Bowden, Peter, Northampton, Enquirer, Dec. 22, 1825, 3
Bowden, Richard, Norfolk, Enquirer, May 31, 1811, 3
Bowden, William, Petersburg, Enquirer, March 3, 1821, 3
Bowe, John, Hanover, Enquirer, Oct. 24, 1823, 3
Bowe, Susanna Davis, Hanover, Whig, July 6, 1838, 1
Bowen, Mrs. Sarah, Culpeper, Whig, April 28, 1830, 3

Bowers, Dr. John L., Southampton, Enquirer, Oct. 6, 1826, 3
Bowler, William C., Richmond, Whig, Nov. 30, 1832, 4
Bowles, Betsy Ann, Hanover, Whig, Aug. 8, 1834, 4
Bowles, Mrs. Elizabeth, Henrico, Enquirer, Feb. 24, 1821, 3
Bowles, Elizabeth Ann, Richmond, Whig, April 1, 1830, 3
⊸Bowles, Lyddal, Henrico, Whig, Nov. 3, 1835, 1
Bowyer, Col. Henry, Fincastle, Whig, June 22, 1832, 3
Boxley, Susannah R., Louisa, Enquirer, July 20, 1827, 3
Boyd, Ann Janetta, Nansemond, Whig, Oct. 26, 1829, 3
Boyd, Durell, Whig, May 12, 1837, 2
Boyd, Mrs. Jane R., Nansemond, Whig, Dec. 11, 1832, 1
Boyd, Mrs. Lucy Ann, New Kent, Whig, Oct. 31, 1834, 1
Boyd, Mrs. Mary, Albemarle, Enquirer, April 24, 1827, 3
Boyd, Mrs. Mary H., King and Queen, Enquirer, Feb. 27, 1821, 3
Boyd, Robert Bolling, New Kent, Whig, Jan. 20, 1837, 2
Boyd, Robert B., King and Queen, Whig, June 22, 1838, 2
Boykin, Francis M., Isle of Wight, Enquirer, Oct. 28, 1817, 3
Boykin, Wm. I., Isle of Wight, Enquirer, Aug. 5, 1823, 3
Boyle, Mrs. Jane, Dumfries, Whig, April 17, 1832, 3
Brack, Mrs. Elizabeth, Richmond, Enquirer, Feb. 14, 1826, 3
Brack, Seth, Richmond, Enquirer, Sept. 2, 1828, 3
Brackett, Capt. Ludwell, Amelia, Enquirer, Dec. 21, 1815, 3
Brackett, Mrs. Martha, Cumberland, Enquirer, July 10, 1818, 3
Brackett, Wilson, Richmond, Whig, Oct. 10, 1837, 2
Bradford, Richard H., Richmond, Whig, April 3, 1835, 3
Bradfute, Davidson, Sweet Springs, Whig, Sept. 12, 1831, 4
Bradish, Wheaton C., Richmond, Whig, Sept. 16, 1834, 2
Bradley, Abraham, Richmond, Whig, May 11, 1838, 2
Bradley, Thomas H., Hampton, Whig, July 14, 1826, 3
Bradly, Spottswood, Henrico, Whig, Aug. 17, 1832, 1
Brady, Patrick H., Giles, Whig, Sept. 10, 1833, 1
Braham, Mrs. Priscilla, Lancaster, Whig, Dec. 11, 1835, 3
Brainham, Mrs. Polly, Columbia, Enquirer, April 2, 1805, 3
Brame, Joseph, Caroline, Enquirer, Nov. 17, 1820, 3
Bramham, Mrs. Augusta, Richmond, Enquirer, June 29, 1824, 3
Bramham, Benjamin, Richmond, Enquirer, March 12, 1814, 3
Bramham, Mrs. Hannah Bushrod, Richmond, Enquirer, Nov. 15, 1814, 3
Branch, Major Bolling, Buckingham, Whig, Nov. 4, 1829, 3
Branch, Mrs. Mary Fleming, ————, Enquirer, Feb. 13, 1817, 3
Branch, Mathew, Powhatan, Enquirer, Oct. 31, 1823, 3
Branch, R. B., Richmond, Enquirer, Feb. 22, 1827, 3
Branch, Thomas, Manchester, Enquirer, Sept. 16, 1828, 3
Branch, William, Prince Edward, Enquirer, Dec. 30, 1825, 3
Brander, Ann Eliza, Manchester, Whig, May 5, 1826, 3
Brander, Everett M., Manchester, Whig, Sept. 27, 1833, 2
Brander, John Murchie, Manchester, Enquirer, Oct. 12, 1821, 3
Branham, Herbert C., Richmond, Whig, Nov. 18, 1836, 4
Bratton, Capt. James, Bath, Enquirer, Sept. 26, 1828, 3
Braxton, Carter, ————, Enquirer, April 14, 1809, 3

Braxton, Mrs. Carter, Richmond, Enquirer, July 9, 1814, 3
Braxton, Mrs. Elizabeth Pope, King William, Whig, Dec. 22, 1831, 3
Braxton, Tayloe, —————, Enquirer, Feb. 21, 1809, 3
Braxton, William Fitzhugh, —————, Enquirer, Jan. 18, 1821, 3
Bray, Ellen, Richmond, Whig, March 13, 1835, 2
Bray, Wm., Richmond, Whig, Oct. 13, 1835, 3
Breckinbridge, Gen. James, Fincastle, Whig, May 24, 1833, 3
Breckenridge, John [Attorney-General of U. S.], Lexington, Enquirer, Jan. 13, 1807, 3
Breckenridge, Mary Ann, Richmond, Whig, Aug. 23, 1830, 3
Brent, Daniel Carroll, Stafford, Enquirer, Jan. 25, 1815, 3
Brent, Richard Fenton, Stafford, Enquirer, Nov. 23, 1824, 3
Bridgeforth, Mrs. Lucy R., Lunenburg, Enquirer, May 6, 1828, 3
Bridges, Richard, Caroline, Enquirer, April 18, 1826, 3
Bridgewater, James, Richmond, Whig, Dec. 15, 1829, 3
Briggs, David, Richmond, Whig, Nov. 8, 25, 1836, 2
Briggs, James, Southampton, Whig, June 28, 1828, 3
Bright, John, Jr., Hardy, Enquirer, Oct. 25, 1822, 3
Bristow, Benj. E., Middlesex, Enquirer, June 1, 1827, 3
Bristow, Robert B., King and Queen, Enquirer, Nov. 23, 1827, 3
Brizendine, Bartlet, Essex, Whig, Nov. 25, 1836, 3
Broach, Wm. Henry, Richmond, Whig, Oct. 17, 1834, 1
Brockenborough, Dr. John, Sr., Essex, Enquirer, Dec. 1, 1804, 3
Brockenbrough, Arthur S., Richmond, Whig, May 1, 1832, 3
Brockenbrough, Mrs. Lettice Lee, Bath, Enquirer, Aug. 29, 1820, 3
Brockenbrough, S[   ], Essex, Enquirer, June 22, 1810, 3
Brockenbrough, Thomas, Richmond, Whig, Oct. 5, 1832, 1
Bronaugh, Dr. John, Dumfries, Enquirer, Nov. 2, 1821, 3
Brooke, Mrs. Humphrey B., Essex, Whig, March 24, 1837, 1
Brooke, Humphrey B., Essex, Enquirer, Dec. 14, 1809, 3
Brooke, John T., Fredericksburg, Enquirer, April 10, 1821, 3
Brooke, John Werth, Essex, Whig, March 24, 1837, 1
Brooke, Capt. Richard, Henrico, Whig, Feb. 6, 1827, 3; Enquirer, Feb. 6, 1827, 3
Brooke, William, —————, Enquirer, May 18, 1821, 3
Brooking, Eliza Randolph, Chesterfield, Enquirer, Sept. 24, 1814, 3
Brooking, Virginia A., Chesterfield, Whig, Sept. 26, 1827, 3
Brooks, Dr. Anson, Richmond, Enquirer, Aug. 22, 1826, 3
Brooks, Sommerville, Richmond, Whig, Oct. 13, 1835, 3
Brotherhood, Mrs. Margaret, Richmond, Whig, March 8, 1838, 2
Brough, Robert, Norfolk, Enquirer, Oct. 17, 1823, 3
Brown, Alexander J., University of Va., Whig, June 10, 1836, 4
Brown, Mrs. Eliza, Richmond, Whig, March 30, 1832, 3
Brown, Mrs. Eliza R., King William, Enquirer, Feb. 18, 1815, 3
Brown, Mrs. Ellen Graham Gordon, Richmond, Whig, May 15, 1838, 1
Brown, George P., Albemarle, Whig, Oct. 17, 1837, 4
Brown, Henry, Jr., Bedford, Whig, June 3, 1836, 4
Brown, Mrs. Isabella McCall, Richmond, Whig, May 26, 1837, 2
Brown, James, Richmond, Whig, May 21, 1833, 2

Brown, James, Richmond, Whig, Jan. 26, 1836, 3
Brown, James, Fredericksburg, Enquirer, May 6, 1808, 3
Brown, James H., Richmond, Whig, Oct. 23, 1832, 2
Brown, John, Richmond, Whig, Jan. 20, 1832, 3
Brown, John, ————, Enquirer, Nov. 29, 1825, 3
Brown, John, Richmond, Enquirer, Nov. 2, 1810, 3
Brown, John, Richmond, Enquirer, Dec. 31, 1822, 3
Brown, Gen. John, Staunton, Whig, Oct. 13, 1826, 3
Brown, John H., Richmond, Enquirer, April 2, 1811, 3
Brown, John Thompson, Petersburg, Whig, Nov. 25, 1836, 3
Brown, Mrs. Lucy, Westmoreland, Whig, Oct. 22, 1829, 3
Brown, Mrs. Martha, Caroline, Enquirer, Dec. 20, 1823, 3
Brown, Mrs. Sarah, James City, Enquirer, Dec. 1, 1826, 3
Browne, Maj. Benjamin Edwards, Surry, Enquirer, May 25, 1819, 3
Browne, Beverly B. ————, Whig, Sept. 10, 1830, 2; Sept. 14, 1830, 3
Browne, Col. John E., Williamsburg, Whig, Jan. 23, 1830, 3
Browne, Louisa A., Williamsburg, Whig, Aug. 24, 1838, 2
Browne, Mrs. Susan, James City, Whig, June 3, 1836, 2
Browne, Wm. B., King William, Whig, Oct. 18, 1833, 1
Bruce, Charles, Halifax, Whig, Jan. 7, 1825, 3
Bruce, Mrs. Elizabeth, Chesterfield, Whig, Sept. 16, 1836, 3
Bruce, James, Halifax, Whig, May 19, 1837, 1
Bruce, Mrs. Sarah, Halifax, Enquirer, May 30, 1806, 3
Brundige, Timothy, Dumfries, Enquirer, Sept. 20, 1822, 3
Bryan, Mrs. E., Richmond, Whig, Nov. 9, 1829, 3
Bryan, William, Richmond, Enquirer, Feb. 6, 1806, 3
Bryan, Capt. Wilson, Richmond, Whig, Nov. 13, 1832, 1
Bryant, Mrs. Jane, Powhatan, Whig, Dec. 29, 1835, 3
Bryant, John, Powhatan, Whig, July 23, 1833, 3
Bryce, Mrs. Ann Smith, Goochland, Enquirer, Jan. 5, 1811, 3
Bryce, Mrs. Louisa S. B., Fredericksburg, Enquirer, Dec. 14, 1822, 3
Bryce, Mrs. Mary, Orange, Enquirer, Oct. 24, 1820, 3
Bryce, Mrs. Sophia, Richmond, Enquirer, April 23, 1817, 3
Buchan, James, Sr., Richmond, Whig, July 11, 1829, 3
Buchanan, Rev. John, Richmond, Enquirer, Dec. 21, 24, 1822, 3
Buckner, Mrs. Ann, Richmond, Whig, May 30, 1837, 2
Buckner, Maj. Colin, Lynchburg, Whig, March 10, 1836, 2
Buckner, George, Caroline, Whig, Nov. 28, 1828, 3
Buckner, Jane, Manchester, Enquirer, June 12, 1816, 3
Buckner, William Horace, Charleston Harbor, Enquirer, Oct. 17, 1820, 3
Buford, Mrs. Martha P., Lunenburg, Enquirer, May 18, 1827, 3
Bullock, Mrs. Ann, Louisa, Whig, July 18, 1826, 3
Bullock, William, Richmond, Enquirer, March 15, 1808, 3
Burch, Mrs. Ann, Richmond, Whig, Dec. 8, 1835, 3
Burch, John, Henrico, Enquirer, Feb. 13, 1817, 3
Burch, Reuben, Lynchburg, Whig, Nov. 8, 1837, 4
Burfoot, Charlotte Matilda, Richmond, Whig, Feb. 2, 1832, 3
Burfoot, John, Chesterfield, Enquirer, Sept. 22, 1826, 3
Burfoot, M. M., Richmond, Whig, July 3, 1827, 3

Burfoot, Mrs. Martha S., Chesterfield, Enquirer, Sept. 24, 1824, 3
Burfoot, Matthew, Richmond, Enquirer, July 3, 1827, 3
Burfoot, Thomas, Chesterfield, Enquirer, Nov. 17, 1820, 3
Burger, Rev. Benjamin, Albemarle, Enquirer, Nov. 22, 1822, 3
Burk, John D., Petersburg, Enquirer, April 2, 19, 1808, 3
Burke, Mrs. Ann Maria, Richmond, Enquirer, April 9, 1822, 3
Burke, Ellen, Richmond, Whig, Nov. 3, 1835, 1
Burke, Thomas, Caroline, Enquirer, Feb. 6, 1807, 3
Burnett, Mrs. Eliza A., Manchester, Whig, April 12, 1836, 3
Burnett, Mrs. Winneyfred, Essex, Whig, Aug. 1, 1837, 2
Burnley, Hardin, Hanover, Enquirer, March 17, 1809, 3
Burnley, James, Louisa, Enquirer, Sept. 8, 1820, 3
Burnley, James, Jr., Louisa, Enquirer, July 30, 1819, 3
Burr, David I., Richmond, Whig, July 20, 1838, 4
Burrows, Mrs. Elizabeth, Richmond, Enquirer, Feb. 17, 1821, 3
Burruss, Capt. Thomas, Caroline, Enquirer, March 19, 1824, 3
Burton, Dr. Aaron, Henrico, Enquirer, Oct. 30, 1821, 3
Burton, Daniel, near Richmond, Enquirer, Sept. 21, 28, 1819, 3
Burton, Mrs. Elizabeth, Richmond, Enquirer, March 30, 1827, 3
Burton, John, Henrico, Whig, Dec. 30, 1828, 3
Burton, Capt. John, Henrico, Whig, May 24, 1828, 3
Burton, Lucy Hardiman, Richmond, Whig, Oct. 3, 1831, 4
Burton, Rebeccah E., Henrico, Enquirer, Sept. 20, 25, 1821, 3
Burton, Capt. Reuben, Henrico, Whig, Aug. 16, 1829, 3
Burton, Robert, Richmond, Enquirer, Feb. 15, 1806, 3
Burton, Samuel Ferdinand, Henrico, Enquirer, Sept. 5, 1817, 3
Burton, Col. Thomas, Richmond, Whig, March 13, 1835, 1
Burton, William F., Henrico, Enquirer, Jan. 15, 1814, 3
Burwell, Mrs. Elizabeth, Mecklenburg, Whig, Dec. 28, 1824, 3; Enquirer,
    Dec. 21, 1824, 3
Burwell, Lewis, Richmond, Whig, Aug. 27, 1833, 1
Burwell, Mrs. Lucy, Botetourt, Enquirer, Nov. 30, 1824, 3
Burwell, Mrs. Mary Hatcher, Manchester, Whig, June 27, 1837, 2
Burwell, Col. Nathaniel, Frederick, Enquirer, April 20, 30, 1814, 3
Burwell, Hon. William A., ————, Enquirer, Feb. 20, 22, 1821, 3
Buskirk, John, Richmond, Whig, Feb. 20, 1838, 1
Butler, Alexander Norman, Louisa, Whig, Sept. 5, 1837, 2
Butler, Benjamin Washington, Hanover, Whig, July 14, 1837, 4
Butler, Mrs. Elizabeth Ann, Richmond, Whig, Sept. 5, 1837, 2
Butler, James E., Richmond, Whig, March 11, 1825, 3
Butler, James M., King and Queen, Whig, April 13, 1838, 2
Butler, Julia Anna, Isle of Wight, Enquirer, July 18, 1826, 3
Butler, Mrs. Mary N., King and Queen, Whig, Sept. 1, 1829, 3
Butler, Mary S., King William, Whig, Sept. 1, 1829, 3
Butler, Mrs. Sarah, Isle of Wight, Enquirer, March 2, 1822, 3
Butler, Thomas, ————, Enquirer, May 7, 1811, 3
Butt, Miles, Manchester, Whig, Oct. 23, 1835, 4
Butts, Mrs. Elizabeth Randolph, Petersburg, Whig, Jan. 17, 1837, 1
Byars, Nr. Wm., Richmond, Enquirer, Aug. 13, 1822, 3

Byrd, Catharine Carter, Gloucester, Whig, May 18, 1838, 4
Byrd, Mrs. Mary, ————, Enquirer, Oct. 8, 1824, 3
Byrd, Richard W., Charles City, Enquirer, Oct. 28, 1815, 3

C.

Cabaniss, James, James City, Whig, April 28, 1837, 2
Cabaniss, Dr. John, Nottoway, Enquirer, Oct. 25, 1822, 3
Cabaniss, Mrs. Minerva, Nottoway, Enquirer, Oct. 25, 1822, 3
Cabell, Ann Carrington, Nelson, Whig, April 20, 1838, 2
Cabell, Dr. George, Richmond, Enquirer, March 1, 1827, 3; Whig, March 2, 1827, 3
Cabell, Mrs. Hannah, Buckingham, Enquirer, Aug. 26, 1817, 3
Cabell, Julia, Richmond, Whig, Dec. 30, 1831, 1
Cabell, Mary Elizabeth, Campbell, Enquirer, May 14, 1822, 3
Cabell, Nicholas C., Richmond, Enquirer, Oct. 19, 1821, 3
Cabell, Patrick, Richmond, Whig, July 6, 1838, 1
Cabell, Dr. Robert B., Chesterfield, Enquirer, Oct. 28, 1808, 3
Cabell, Col. William, Nelson, Enquirer, Dec. 12, 1822, 3
Cahoon, Mrs. Ann, Suffolk, Enquirer, July 15, 1823, 3
Cahoon, Gen. John C., Norfolk, Enquirer, Oct. 24, 1823, 3
Caldwell, James, Culpeper, Whig, Aug. 21, 1832, 3
Callaway, Nelson, Nelson, Whig, Feb. 23, 1838, 4
Calleway, Dr. George, Nelson, Enquirer, Oct. 8, 1822, 3
Callis, Col. William Overton, Louisa, Enquirer, June 8, 1814, 3
Callomb, Samuel, Pittsylvania, Enquirer, Nov. 18, 1808, 3
Cammack, Eliza, Spottsylvania, Whig, Feb. 6, 1838, 2
Camp, Col. George Washington, Norfolk, Enquirer, Dec. 11, 1823, 3
Campbell, Anna Louise, Williamsburg, Enquirer, Nov. 12, 1822, 3
Campbell, Archibald, Richmond, Whig, Dec. 1, 1830, 2
Campbell, Charles, Richmond, Whig, Dec. 23, 1825, 3
Campbell, Edward, Washington, Whig, March 12, 1833, 3
Campbell, John, Washington and Augusta, Enquirer, Jan. 3, 5, 1825, 3
Campbell, Mrs. Phanuel, Albemarle, Whig, June 28, 1833, 2
Campbell, Susan Gatliff, Williamsburg, Enquirer, Nov. 12, 1822, 3
Campbell, Thos. R., King and Queen, Whig, March 8, 1833, 3
Campbell, Col. William, Orange, Enquirer, Nov. 11, 1823, 3
Canby, Wm., ————, Whig, Sept. 28, 1832, 1
Cantor, Reuben, Richmond, Whig, July 2, 1828, 3
Cantor, Reuben, Lancaster, Enquirer June 24, 1828, 3
Cargill, Nathaniel, Sussex, Whig, May 8, 1827, 3
Carpenter, Charles W., Richmond, Whig, March 25, 1829, 3
Carpenter, Meriwether, Louisa, Enquirer, Oct. 20, 1820, 3
Carr, Dabney, Richmond, Whig, Jan. 10, 1837, 2
Carr, Dabney Overton, Albemarle, Whig, Dec. 13, 1830, 3
Carr, Mrs. Eleanor B., Albemarle, Enquirer, July 15, 1815, 3
Carr, Elizabeth, Martinsburg, Whig, June 5, 1838, 4
Carr, Col. John, Albemarle, Enquirer, Oct. 8, 1824, 3
Carr, John A., Albemarle, Whig, May 19, 1837, 3

Carr, Mrs. Maria, Albemarle, Whig, Dec. 4, 1832, 1
Carr, Martha, Albemarle, Enquirer, Sept. 13, 1811, 3
Carr, Peter, Albemarle, Enquirer, March 1, 4, 1815, 3
Carrington, Col. Edward, Richmond, Enquirer, Oct. 30, 1810, 3; Nov. 2, 1810, 3
Carrington, Gen. George, Halifax, Enquirer, June 6, 1809, 3
Carrington, John A., Richmond, Whig, Sept. 12, 1831, 4
Carrington, John A., Richmond, Whig, Aug. 14, 1832, 1
Carrington, John M., Richmond, Whig, Jan. 13, 1832, 3
Carrington, Margaret Ann, Richmond, Whig, April 21, 1835, 3
Carrington, Judge Paul, Charlotte, Enquirer, Jan. 23, 1816, 3
Carrington, Paul I., Cumberland, Whig, March 28, 1826, 3
Carrington, Richard A., Richmond, Whig, Jan. 13, 1832, 3
Carson, Caroline Matilda, Powhatan, Whig, Nov. 15, 1833, 1
Carter, Mrs. Ann, "Shirley," Enquirer, April 28, 1809, 3
Carter, Mrs. Betty, Frederick, Whig, April 27, 1830, 3
Carter, Charles, Pittsylvania, Whig, June 1, 1827, 3
Carter, Dr. Charles, Corottoman, Enquirer, Dec. 20, 1825, 3
Carter, Charles, "Shirley," Enquirer, July 22, 1806, 3
Carter, Mrs. Charlotte, Richmond, Enquirer, July 30, 1822, 3
Carter, Elizabeth Landon, Fairfax, Whig, Oct. 21, 1836, 1
Carter, Mrs. Elizabeth M., "Sabine Hall," Whig, April 6, 1832, 1
Carter, Ellen M. Bankhead, Albemarle, Whig, Jan. 19, 1838, 1
Carter, Isaetta, Albemarle, Enquirer, May 14, 1824, 3
Carter, Joseph A., Lancaster, Whig, Feb. 20, 1838, 1
Carter, Landon, "Sabine Hall," Enquirer, Sept. 15, 1820, 3
Carter, Mrs. Lucy, Richmond, Whig, May 2, 1837, 2
Carter, Mrs. Maria V., Goochland, Whig, June 30, 1835, 4
Carter, Mrs. Martha H., near Richmond, Whig, Dec. 4, 1829, 3
Carter, Mary Martha, Richmond, Whig, July 7, 1837, 2
Carter, Robert E., King and Queen, Enquirer, March 5, 1814, 3
Carter, Rowena G., Richmond, Whig, Dec. 5, 1837, 2
Carter, Capt. Samuel, Prince Edward, Whig, May 8, 1830, 3
Carter, Mrs. Sarah, Fauquier, Enquirer, June 1, 1827, 3
Carter, Mrs. St. Leger L. [Mary Elizabeth], King George, Whig, Feb. 10, 1837, 2
Carter, Thomas J., Gloucester, Enquirer, March 23, 1821, 3
Carter, Thomas W., Richmond, Whig, Feb. 2, 1836, 1
Cartmill, Col. James, Buchanan, Whig, Dec. 30, 1836, 4
Caruthers, Alexander, Fluvanna, Whig, Jan. 19, 1838, 1
Caruthers, William, Lexington, Enquirer, June 20, 1817, 3
Cary, Mrs. Ann Wythe, Hampton, Enquirer, Nov. 1, 1822, 3
Cary, Cyrus, ——————, Whig, April 20, 1832, 1
Cary, Jane, Williamsburg, Enquirer, July 19, 1805, 3
Cary, Capt. John, Gloucester, Enquirer, Feb. 11, 1823, 3
Cary, Mrs. Mary, Chesterfield, Whig, March 24, 1836, 3
Cary, Col. Miller, Fluvanna, Enquirer, Jan. 3, 1828, 3
Cary, Sarah, Yorktown, Enquirer, Dec. 3, 1811, 3
Cary, Wilson Jefferson, Fluvanna, Enquirer, Oct. 3, 1823, 3

Cary, Wilson Miles, Fluvanna, Enquirer, Dec. 4, 1817, 3
Catlett, Agnes, Gloucester, Whig, June 22, 1838, 2
Catlett, Caroline, King William, Enquirer, Oct. 17, 1823, 3
Catlin, Mrs. Elizabeth, Richmond, Whig, Feb. 8, 1833, 3
Cayce, Mrs. Ann, Charlotte, Enquirer, Feb. 9, 1822, 3
Chaffin, Maj. Joshua, Amelia, Enquirer, April 23, 1824, 3
Chaigneau, Jean Pierre Benjamin, Richmond, Enquirer, July 2, 1813, 1
Chamberlain, Charlotte, Richmond, Whig, Aug. 16, 1833, 1
Chamberlayne, Alfred D., Richmond, Whig, May 1, 1835, 1
Chamberlayne, Edward P., King William, Enquirer, June 17, 1806, 3
Chamberlayne, Rebecca Mosby, Richmond, Whig, Aug. 12, 1829, 3
Chamberlayne, Mrs. Sarah, King William, Enquirer, Sept. 9, 1828, 3
Chamberlayne, Gen. William, New Kent, Whig, Sept. 6, 1836, 2
Chamberlayne, Wm. M., Henrico, Whig, June 15, 1838, 2
Chandler, Dwight Backers, Caroline, Enquirer, Sept. 18, 1821, 3
Chandler, Mrs. Eloisa R., Louisa, Enquirer, Feb. 14, 1824, 3
Chandler, James, New Kent, Enquirer, Sept. 10, 1813, 3
Chandler, Mrs. Lucy, Richmond, Whig, April 7, 1835, 4
Chandler, Timothy, Caroline, Whig, March 30, 1831, 1
Chaudoin, Mrs. Catherine, Goochland, Enquirer, Nov. 9, 1821, 3
Chapell, John, Halifax, Enquirer, Oct. 25, 1825, 3
Chaplin, Wm. R., Danville, Whig, Aug. 23, 1833, 1
Chapman, Mrs. Jane B., Gloucester, Whig, June 9, 1837, 2
Chapman, Mrs. Mary Gabriella, Richmond, Whig, July 4, 1837, 2
Chappell, Carrell F., New Kent, Whig, Oct. 26, 1830, 3
Charter, Nathaniel, Richmond, Whig, July 21, 1837, 1
Chase, Judge Samuel, —————, Enquirer, June 25, 1811, 2
Chestein, Rev. Rainey, Buckingham, Enquirer, Nov. 21, 1823, 3
Chatham, Mrs. Nancy C., Charlotte, Enquirer, March 16, 1824, 3
Chauncey, Capt. Wolcott, Richmond, Whig, Nov. 3, 1835, 1
Cheadle, Mrs. Elizabeth, Prince Edward, Enquirer, Dec. 9, 1823, 3
Cheatham, Eugenia P., Manchester, Enquirer, May 17, 1825, 3
Cheatham, Mrs. Martha, Richmond, Whig, July 15, 1834, 3
Cheatham, Col. Matthew, Chesterfield, Enquirer, Nov. 1, 1815, 3
Cheatham, Mrs. Nancy C., Charlotte, Enquirer, March 16, 1824, 3
Cheatham, Capt. Thomas, Chesterfield, Whig, Sept. 22, 1827, 3
Cheatham, William, Charlotte, Enquirer, Oct. 17, 1823, 3
Chesebrough, E., Richmond, Enquirer, June 28, 1825, 3
Chevallie, Elizabeth, Richmond, Whig, Jan. 8, 1833, 3
Chevalli, John Augustus, Richmond, Whig, June 12, 1838, 2
Chevernet, Mary Ann, Richmond, Whig, Oct. 20, 1831, 1
Chew, Claiborne, Richmond, Enquirer, Feb. 4, 1817, 3
Chew, Robert S., Fredericksburg, Enquirer, Nov. 7, 1826, 3
Chewning, Mrs. Jamima, Louisa, Enquirer, Nov. 16, 1827, 2
Childers, Margaret H., Richmond, Whig, Aug. 9, 1830, 2
Childers, Nathaniel, Hanover, Whig, April 5, 1836, 3
Chinn, Dr. John Yates, Richmond, Enquirer, Aug. 11, 1826, 3
Chowning, Julia Ann Carter, Middlesex, Whig, March 8, 1833, 3
Christian, Betsy Collier, Craighton, Whig, Sept. 12, 1831, 3

Christian, Edward Warren, Charles City, Whig, Oct. 3, 1834, 1
Christian, Elizabeth Jane, Princess Ann, Enquirer, Feb. 21, 1824, 3
Christian, James R., New Kent, Whig, May 13, 1834, 2
Christian, Dr. Jordon C., Charles City, Whig, May 15, 1835, 2
Christian, Capt. Joseph, Charles City, Enquirer, April 26, 1825, 3
Christian, Mrs. Lucy J. W., Buckingham, Enquirer, Aug. 17, 1824, 3
Christian, Mrs. Martha, Buckingham, Enquirer, Sept. 8, 1820, 3
Christian, Mrs. Martha, Williamsburg, Whig, Feb. 16, 1838, 4
Christian, Robert, New Kent, Enquirer, Aug. 6, 1822, 3
Christian, Susan, New Kent, Enquirer, Sept. 12, 1817, 3
Christian, Warren, Charles City, Enquirer, March 19, 1811, 3
Church, A., Ashby's Mill, Enquirer, June 20, 1826, 2
Claiborne, Mrs. Delia, Richmond, Whig, Aug. 3, 1838, 2
Claiborne, Mrs. Euphania, King and Queen, Whig, May 1, 1832, 3
Claiborne, Ferdinand Leigh, ——————, Enquirer, April 26, 1815, 3
Claiborne, Mrs. Frances, King William, Enquirer, June 18, 1819, 3
Claiborne, Hon. John, Brunswick, Enquirer, Oct. 21, 1808, 2
Claiborne, Mrs. Mary Leigh, Powhatan, Enquirer, Oct. 18, 1814, 3
Claiborne, Virginia Herbert, Richmond, Whig, May 21, 1830, 3
Claiborne, William, ——————, Enquirer, Oct. 3, 1809, 3
Claiborne, Wm. Dandridge, King William, Enquirer, June 18, 1811, 3
Claiborne, Dr. William Presley, King William, Enquirer, Aug. 1, 1817, 3
Clapham, Samuel, Loudoun, Whig, Sept. 19, 1826, 3
Clark, Caroline Virginia, Albemarle, Whig, Sept. 18, 1832, 2
Clark, Carter, Mecklenburg, Enquirer, Jan. 5, 1828, 3
Clark, Mrs. Elizabeth, near Richmond, Enquirer, July 15, 1806, 3
Clark, Glovina Geraldine, Richmond, Whig, July 15, 1834, 3
Clark, John, Halifax, Enquirer, March 27, 1827, 3
Clark, Micajah, Sr., Albemarle, Enquirer, Aug. 2, 1808, 3
Clark, Wm. Dodge Adams, Charlottesville, Enquirer, Sept. 5, 1828, 3
Clark, Wm., Pittsylvania, Enquirer, April 17, 1827, 3
Clark, Col. William S., Pittsylvania C. H., Enquirer, Feb. 8, 1821, 3
Clarke, Mrs. Betsy, Richmond, Whig, April 10, 1835, 2
Clarke, Dr. George, Essex, Enquirer, Oct. 15, 1822, 3
Clarke, James, Williamsburg, Whig, Nov. 25, 1825, 3
Clarke, Col. James, Powhatan, Whig, Jan. 3, 1831, 3
Clarke, James, Jr., Manchester, Enquirer, Aug. 14, 1816, 3
Clarke, John, Richmond, Whig, Feb. 9, 1829, 3
Clarke, Joseph, Buckingham, Enquirer, Jan. 25, 1814, 1
Clarke, Mrs. Margaret J., Chesterfield, Whig, Sept. 30, 1836, 2
Clarke, Mrs. Mary Ann, Powhatan, Enquirer, Sept. 12, 1807, 3
Clarke, Milton, Manchester, Whig, Oct. 3, 1834, 1
Clarke, Richard, Nelson, Whig, March 8, 1836, 3
Clarke, Mrs. Sarah, Buckingham, Enquirer, Aug. 31, 1827, 3
Clarke, Washington Irvin, Richmond, Whig, Nov. 13, 1835, 2
Clarke, William, Hanover, Enquirer, Dec. 16, 1826, 3
Clarke, Wm., Powhatan, Whig, April 6, 1831, 1
Clarkson, James, Essex, Enquirer, Oct. 8, 1824, 3
Clarkson, Thomas, Essex, Whig, April 30, 1833, 2

Claudoin, Mrs. Catherine, Goochland, Enquirer, Nov. 9, 1821, 3
Clay, Mrs. Mary, Chesterfield, Enquirer, Sept. 2, 1825, 3
Clay, Matthew, Campbell, Enquirer, June 10, 1815, 3
Clay, Matthew, Lawrence, Enquirer, March 3, 1827, 3
Clay, Capt. Samuel, Chesterfield, Whig, Feb. 1, 1831, 1
Claybrooke, Mrs. Sarah, Louisa, Enquirer, Sept. 24, 1822, 3
Clements, Mrs. Louisa, Tappahannock, Enquirer, Dec. 20, 1823, 3
Clements, Mrs. Sarah, Amelia, Enquirer, Oct. 19, 1821, 3
Clency, Michael, Goochland, Whig, July 6, 1824, 4
Clifford, Elizabeth, Richmond, Whig, May 19, 1830, 2
Clopton, Patrick, Bowling Green, Whig, July 23, 1829, 3
Clopton, Mrs. Robert [Frances], Pittsylvania, Whig, April 18, 1837, 2
Clopton, Dr. Waldegrave, ————, Whig, Nov. 30, 1832, 4
Coalter, John, near Fredericksburg, Whig, Feb. 9, 1838, 4
Coats, John, Richmond, Whig, August 18, 1831, 3
Cobbs, Mrs. Mary, Buckingham, Whig, April 27, 1832, 1,
Cobbs, Capt. Nicholas, Buckingham, Enquirer, Oct. 31, 1823, 3
Cobbs, Capt. Robert, Campbell, Whig, Sept. 7, 1829, 3
Cocke, Mrs. ————, Albemarle, Whig, Oct. 31, 1834, 2
Cocke, Bowler F., Henrico, Enquirer, June 10, 1825, 3
Cocke, Mrs. Jane S., Amelia, Whig, April 14, 1835, 3
Cocke, Mrs. John Hartwell, ————, Enquirer, Jan. 14, 1817, 3
Cocke, John Lewis, Powhatan, Whig, June 3, 1825, 3; Enquirer, June 3, 1825, 2
Cocke, Mrs. Maria, Henrico, Enquirer, April 1, 1806, 3
Cocke, Maria Carter, Cumberland, Enquirer, Jan. 31, 1824, 3
Cocke, Richard, Henrico, Enquirer, May 26, 1820, 3
Cocke, Col. Richard, Isle of Wight, Enquirer, Feb. 17, 30, 1816, 3
Cocke, Robert, Richmond, Whig, May 5, 1837, 2
Cocke, Thomas, Surry, Enquirer, May 2, 1822, 3
Cocke, Wm., Cumberland, Enquirer, April 22, 1828, 3
Cocke, Capt. Wm. A., Powhatan, Enquirer, Sept. 7, 1821, 3
Cocke, William H., ————, Enquirer, April 11, 1823, 3
Coe, Mrs. Frances Caroline, Richmond, Whig, Oct. 29, 1833, 2
Cogbile, Nelson, ————, Enquirer, May 9, 1806, 3
Cohen, Jacob J. [formerly of Richmond], Enquirer, Oct. 17, 1823, 3
Cohoon, Mrs. Ann, Suffolk, Enquirer, July 15, 1823, 3
Cohoon, Gen. John C., Norfolk, Enquirer, Oct. 24, 1823, 3
Coke, John, Williamsburg, Enquirer, April 16, 1822, 3
Coke, Mrs. Lucy, Williamsburg, Enquirer, Nov. 10, 1810, 3
Coke, Mrs. Mary, Williamsburg, Whig, Oct. 10, 1831, 2
Cole, Frances Catharine, Fluvanna, Enquirer, Aug. 13, 1824, 3
Cole, Mrs. Frances C., Fluvanna, Enquirer, Jan. 20, 1814, 3
Cole, Hamblin, Chesterfield, Whig, July 28, 1837, 2
Cole, James, Jr., Fluvanna, Enquirer, Feb. 6, 1812, 3
Cole, Mrs. Mary, Richmond, Whig, Nov. 17, 1837, 2
Coleman, Mrs. Ann, Fredericksburg, Whig, Aug. 14, 1832, 1
Coleman, Mrs. Ann, Halifax, Enquirer, June 18, 1824, 3
Coleman, Mrs. Ann, Nelson, Enquirer, March 18, 1828, 3

Coleman, B. W., Richmond, Enquirer, Oct. 17, 1823, 3
Coleman, Mrs. Elizabeth, Halifax, Enquirer, Sept. 5, 1826, 3
Coleman, Marcia E., Caroline, Whig, Aug. 22, 1834, 1
Coleman, Peter G., Caroline, Enquirer, March 28, 1820, 3
Coleman, Mrs. Susanna, ————, Enquirer, Nov. 29, 1815, 3
Coleman, Thomas G., Louisa, Whig, Sept. 2, 1825, 3
Coleman, William, Williamsburg, Enquirer, Dec. 21, 1819, 3
Coleman, Wm. B., Spottsylvania, Enquirer, Jan. 30, 1827, 3
Coles, Isaac, Pittsylvania, Enquirer, July 13, 1813, 4
Coles, Isaac H., Halifax, Enquirer, Feb. 23, 1814, 3
Coles, Mrs. Louisa G., Norfolk, Enquirer, Sept. 10, 1824, 3
Collier, Charles M., Elizabeth City, Whig, May 4, 1827, 3
Collins, Thomas, Essex, Whig, May 30, 1837, 1
Colquhoun, Sutherland, Richmond, Whig, Dec. 4, 1832, 1
Colquitt, Thomas, Powhatan, Whig, Aug. 21, 1838, 4
Colston, John J. M., ————, Enquirer, Nov. 22, 1825, 3
Colston, Rawleigh, Berkley, Enquirer, Aug. 15, 1823, 3
Colton, Josephus B., ————, Whig, Sept. 7, 1829, 3
Colton, Mrs. Lilly F., Richmond, Whig, June 28, 1833, 1
Comner, Capt. Francis, Norfolk, Whig, May 5, 1835, 3
Conroy, Mrs. and five children, ————, Enquirer, May 6, 1825, 1
Converse, John Thornton, Richmond, Whig, Feb. 25, 1831, 3
Conway, Capt. Catlett, Orange, Enquirer, Sept. 11, 1827, 3
Conway, Mrs. Harriet, Orange, Enquirer, May 6, 1825, 3
Conway, Thomas B., Richmond, Whig, Dec. 16, 1825, 3; Enquirer, Dec.
    10, 1825, 3
Cook, Francis S., Richmond, Whig, Sept. 2, 1834, 3
Cook, John L., Richmond, Whig, April 26, 1836, 1
Cooke, Mrs. Agatha Eliza, Stafford, Whig, July 30, 1833, 1
Cooke, Hannah, Stafford, Whig, Sept. 5, 1826, 3
Cooke, John, Gloucester, Enquirer, March 13, 18, 1823, 3
Cooke, Maria, Stafford, Whig, Dec. 9, 1831, 1
Cooke, Samuel M., Gloucester, Enquirer, April 5, 1808, 3
Cooke, Thomas, Portsmouth, Enquirer, Oct. 20, 1818, 3
Cooke, William, Richmond, Whig, Aug. 11, 1837, 2
Cooke, Wm. Powhatan, Smithfield, Enquirer, Oct. 7, 1823, 3
Cooksey, Edward, Waterford, Enquirer, Aug. 10, 1821, 3
Cooksey, George, Waterford, Enquirer, Aug. 10, 1821, 3
Cooksey, Harrison, Waterford, Enquirer, Aug. 10, 1821, 3
Cooley, Wm. S., Prince Edward, Whig, July 4, 1833, 3
Cooper, Elvira, Richmond, Enquirer, Dec. 27, 1817, 3
Copeland, Elisha, Nansemond, Whig, Aug. 19, 1829, 3
Copeland, Hennengham C., Richmond, Whig, July 31, 1838, 2
Copeland, Margaret, Richmond, Enquirer, Jan. 7, 1812, 3
Copland, Mrs. Charles, Richmond, Whig, Nov. 29, 1836, 1
Corbin, Mrs. Caroline Rebecca Heath, Whig, Oct. 23, 1829, 3
Corbin, Francis, Caroline, Enquirer, June 1, 1821, 3
Corbin, Maj. Garwin L., York, Enquirer, June 29, 1813, 3
Corbin, John, Lanesville, ————, Enquirer, Jan. 11, 1816, 3

Corbin, Mrs. Rebecca Park, King and Queen, Enquirer, April 26, 1822, 3
Corbin, Richard C., Caroline, Whig, Dec. 16, 1825, 3
Corbin, Maj. Richard, King and Queen, Enquirer, June 18, 1819, 3
Corwin, James H., Richmond, Whig, April 30, 1830, 3
Cosby, Capt. Duke, Louisa, Enquirer, Sept. 7, 1819, 3
Cosby, Minor M., Albemarle, Enquirer, Feb. 23, 1810, 3
Cottom, Samuel, Richmond, Whig, July 7, 1826, 3
Cottrell, Peter, Henrico, Enquirer, March 1, 1827, 3
Couch, John R., Mason, Whig, Oct. 17, 1834, 1
Couch, Margaret, Goochland, Whig, Sept. 1, 1829, 3
Couch, William, Petersburg, Enquirer, Jan. 27, 1821, 3
Coulling, Rev. James, ————, Enquirer, Oct. 7, 1807, 3
Coupland, Carter, Petersburg, Whig, June 18, 1832, 4
Courtney, Mrs. Jane, Richmond, Enquirer, March 22, 1808, 3
Courtney, John, Richmond, Whig, Dec. 21, 1824, 3
Courtney, Mary C., Richmond, Whig, May 7, 1829, 3
Courtney, Philip W., [formerly of Virginia], Whig, Aug. 30, 1836, 4
Courtney, Philip, King and Queen, Enquirer, Feb. 24, 1809, 3
Courtney, Mrs. Susannah, Richmond, Enquirer, July 8, 1815, 3
Cousins, Martha E. S., Amelia, Enquirer, Oct. 4, 1815, 3
Cousins, Richard Henry, Pittsylvania, Whig, July 12, 1828, 3
Coventry, Robert, ————, Enquirer, March 11, 1817, 3
Cowherd, Albert G., Louisa, Enquirer, Aug. 12, 1823, 3
Cowland, Rev. James, Richmond, Enquirer, Sept. 26, 1806, 3
Cowling, Mrs. E. N., ————, Enquirer, Dec. 14, 1822, 3
Cowling, Mrs. Matilda, Richmond, Whig, Aug. 9, 1828, 3
Cowling, Willis, Richmond, Whig, Aug. 20, 1828, 3; Enquirer, Aug. 22, 1828, 3
Cox, Charles, Sr., Richmond, Enquirer, April 9, 1811, 3
Cox, David, Richmond, Whig, June 6, 1837, 3
Cox, Edward Thomas, Chesterfield, Enquirer, Aug. 21, 1827, 3
Cox, Mrs. Mary, Chesterfield, Enquirer, June 15, 1827, 3
Cox, Wm. Herbert, Richmond, Whig, Oct. 24, 1831, 2
Craddock, George, Amelia, Enquirer, Feb. 20, 1816, 3
Crafton, William B., New Kent, Whig, June 15, 1838, 2
Craig, Adam, Richmond, Enquirer, May 14, 1808, 8
Craig, John J., Staunton, Whig, Jan. 16, 1838, 1
Crawford, Irvin, Richmond, Whig, Nov. 4, 1829, 3
Crawford, John, Louisa, Enquirer, April 24, 1827, 3
Crawford, Peter, Louisa, Enquirer, March 8, 1827, 3
Crenshaw, Charles, Hanover, Whig, Nov. 1, 1825, 3; Enquirer, Nov. 1, 1825, 3
Crenshaw, Charles T., Richmond, Whig, April 1, 1829, 3
Crenshaw, David, Bedford, Whig, Feb. 14, 1830, 3
Crenshaw, John, Hanover, Enquirer, March 10, 1818, 3
Crenshaw, Louisa, Richmond, Whig, Feb. 4, 1832, 1,
Crenshaw, Mrs. Mary T., Richmond, Whig, March 6, 1827, 3
Crenshaw, Mrs. Sarah, Hanover, Enquirer, Feb. 3, 1816, 3
Crew, Eleazer, Charles City, Enquirer, Nov. 19, 1822, 3

Crew, James, Richmond, Whig, Nov. 16, 1832, 4
Crews, Jesse, Louisa, Enquirer, Dec. 29, 1826, 3
Crissy, Moses, Prince Edward, Enquirer, May 14, 1822, 3
Crittenden, Mary Y., Richmond, Whig, May 8, 1835, 3
Crittenden, Robert, Surry, Enquirer, Feb. 10, 1821, 3
Crittenden, Mrs. Sarah C., Middlesex, Enquirer, Jan. 31, 1824, 3
Crittenden, Capt. Zachariah U., Middlesex, Enquirer, Jan. 27, 1827, 3
Crocker, Mrs. Clarissa, —————, Enquirer, June 5, 1821, 3
Cropper, Gen. John, Bowman's Folly, Enquirer, Jan. 30, 1821, 3
Cross, Mrs. Betty Ann, Hanover, Enquirer, Sept. 1, 1820, 3
Cross, Fleming B., Hanover, Whig, Oct. 7, 1830, 3
Cross, Rev. Joseph, Goochland, Enquirer, March 9, 1814, 3
Crouch, Frances Trent, Richmond, Whig, Sept. 28, 1832, 1
Crouch, Dr. John G., Henrico, Whig, June 20, 1837, 1
Crouch, Joseph Trent, Richmond, Whig, Sept. 28, 1832, 1
Crouch, Richard, Sr., —————, Enquirer, May 14, 1811, 3
Crouch, Richard, Richmond, Enquirer, Oct. 28, 1808, 3
Crow, Martha, King and Queen, Whig, Aug. 9, 1836, 4
Crozet, Adele, Richmond, Whig, March 8, 1830, 3
Crump, Mrs. Amelia, Manchester, Enquirer, Oct. 21, 1817, 3
Crump, Benedict, New Kent, Whig, Aug. 1, 1937, 2
Crump, Beverly, New Kent, Whig, March 7, 1837, 3; Feb. 28, 1837, 3
Crump, Mrs. Mary F., —————, Enquirer, Feb. 25, 1826, 3
Crump, Mrs. Parthinia, New Kent, Whig, Feb. 28, 1833, 1
Crump, Col. Richard, Powhatan, Enquirer, May 4, 1813, 3
Crumpler, Merit, [formrly of Smithfield], Whig, April 4, 1837, 1
Crutchfield, John, Hanover, Whig, July 25, 1834, 1
Crutchfield, Ralph, Richmond, Whig, Nov. 15, 1833, 1
Cryer, Mrs. Sarah, Surry, Whig, Oct. 3, 1831, 4
Cullen, Mary Eliza, Richmond, Whig, May 1, 1838, 2
Cunliffe, John, Chesterfield, Enquirer, June 29, 1824, 3
Cunningham, Edward, Sr., Goochland, Whig, March 18, 1836, 3
Cunningham, Mrs. Eliza C., Howard's Neck, Enquirer, Oct. 24, 1826, 3
Cunningham, Richard M., Richmond, Whig, July 7, 1831, 3
Cunningham, Robert Marshall, Mecklenburg, Whig, Aug. 16, 1836, 2
Cunningham, William, Hanover, Whig, June 27, 1831, 4
Cunnington, Humphrey, Richmond, Whig, Nov. 12, 1833, 1
Curd, Mrs. Anne, Goochland, Whig, April 28, 1826, 3
Curd, Mrs. Caroline R., Goochland, Enquirer, July 13, 1816, 3
Curd, Col. John, Goochland, Enquirer, March 23, 1819, 3
Cureton, James, Petersburg, Enquirer, July 13, 1813, 1
Currie, Dr. James, Richmond, Enquirer, April 24, 1807, 3
Currie, James, —————, Whig, Aug. 10, 1832, 3
Curtis, Maj. Charles, Gloucester, Enquirer, Dec. 22, 1807, 3
Curtis, Mrs. Harriet Ann, Richmond, Whig, Aug. 15, 1837, 2
Curtis, John Foushee, Hanover, Whig, Jan. 16, 1835, 4
Cushing, Jonathan P., Prince Edward, Whig, May 19, 1835, 1
Cushman, Ellen Weld, Richmond, Whig, April 19, 1830, 3
Custis, Mrs. Eliza Park, Richmond, Whig, Jan. 3, 1832, 3

Cutler, Mrs. Susan, Dinwiddie, Whig, Jan. 3, 1837, 3
Cutler, Dr. Wm., Dinwiddie, Whig, May 27, 1836, 2
Cutting, Mrs. Sally Carter, Stafford, Enquirer, May 4, 1814, 3

D.

Dabney, Mrs. Ann, Richmond, Whig, Aug. 22, 1834, 1
Dabney, Augustine, Gloucester, Whig, June 8, 1830, 3
Dabney, Benj., King William, Enquirer, Dec. 23, 1826, 3; Whig, Dec. 29, 1826, 3
Dabney, Dr. Benj. F., Gloucester, Whig, Aug. 4, 1837, 2
Dabney, Mrs. Diana, King William, Enquirer, Aug. 24, 1824, 3
Dabney, Mrs. Eliza, Caroline, Enquirer, May 4, 1827, 3
Dabney, George, Hanover, Enquirer, Aug. 25, 1818, 3
Dabney, Maj. George, King William, Enquirer, Jan. 9, 1828, 3
Dabney, George H., King William, Whig, Sept. 23, 1834, 4
Dabney, Henry T., King William, Whig, Sept. 23, 1829, 3
Dabney, Mrs. Jemima G., Cumberland, Enquirer, March 23, 1821, 3
Dabney, John, Lynchburg, Enquirer, May 18, 1816, 3
Dabney, John B., Richmond, Enquirer, Nov. 10, 1826, 3
Dabney, Mrs. Lucy Ann, Powhatan, Whig, April 4, 1834, 3
Dabney, Richard, Louisa, Enquirer, Nov. 25, 1825, 3
Dabney, Mrs. Susan L., King William, Whig, April 27, 1827, 3
Dabney, Mrs. Susan S., King William, Enquirer, May 1, 1827, 3
Dabney, William, Louisa, Whig, April 4, 1837, 1
Dabney, Wm., Richmond, Enquirer, Feb. 26, 1822, 3
Dade, Wm. A. G., Prince William, Whig, Oct. 22, 1829, 3
Daily, James, Romney, Enquirer, Oct. 3, 1823, 3
Daingerfield, Ann C., Tappahannock, Whig, Oct. 10, 1937, 4
Daingerfield, Mrs. Eleanor Bowles, Tappahannock, Enquirer, July 25, 1826, 3
Dance, Harrison, Richmond, Enquirer, June 6, 1823, 3
Dandridge, Bartholomew, New Kent, Enquirer, Jan. 18, 1827, 3
Dandridge, Julius B., Richmond, Whig, April 26, 1828, 3; Enquirer, April 29, 1828, 3
Dandridge, Mrs. Santa Maria, Richmond, Enquirer, Aug. 3, 1824, 3
Danforth, Sarah King, Richmond, Enquirer, July 28, 1826, 3
Dangerfield, Col. Wm. A., near Alexander, Enquirer, Nov. 30, 1821, 3
Daniel, Col. Chisley, Charlotte, Enquirer, Feb. 5, 1822, 3
Daniel, Eliza Travers, Stafford, Enquirer, Nov. 11, 1823, 3
Daniel, Frances, Stafford, Enquirer, April 14, 1820, 3
Daniel, Dr. John Moncure, Stafford, Enquirer, Oct. 22, 1813, 4
Daniel, Mrs. Margaret, Falmouth, Enquirer, March 14, 1809, 3
Daniel, Walter Raleigh, Stafford, Enquirer, Sept. 19, 1828, 3
Darmsdatt, Joseph, Richmond, Enquirer, Jan. 4, 1820, 3
Darracott, John, Hanover, Whig, July 19, 1836, 1
Darracott, Mrs. Susanna, Hanover, Whig, Aug. 1, 1831, 4
Dasory, Mrs. Celia W., Gloucester, Whig, Oct. 27, 1837, 2
Davenport, Mrs. Frances, Richmond, Enquirer, Jan. 25, 1816, 3

Davidson, David, [formerly of Richmond], Whig, Aug. 11, 1831, 4
Davidson, Edward, Buckingham, Enquirer, May 1, 1827, 3
Davidson, Mrs. Mary, Charlotte, Enquirer, Jan. 6, 1827, 3
Davidson, William, Richmond, Enquirer, May 16, 1809, 3
Davies, Mrs. Emma, Buckingham, Whig, May 15, 1835, 4
Davis, Mrs. Ann, Richmond, Whig, Nov. 3, 1837, 2
Davis, Augustine, Yorktown, Whig, Nov. 4, 1825, 3
Davis, Edward C., Richmond, Enquirer, Jan. 1, 1822, 3
Davis, John, ————, Enquirer, Sept. 16, 1806, 3
Davis, Col. Joseph B., Powhatan, Whig, April 26, 1834, 3
Davis, Mrs. Lucy, Gloucester, Enquirer, Oct. 31, 1823, 3
Davis, Mrs. Martha, Richmond, Whig, Nov. 15, 1825, 3; Enquirer, Nov.
    15, 1825, 3
Davis, Mary, Richmond, Enquirer, June 4, 1811, 3
Davis, Mrs. Peggy, King and Queen, Whig, Feb. 11, 1832, 3
Davis, Rev. Thomas, Norfolk, Enquirer, Dec. 14, 1815, 3
Davis, Robert C. [formerly of Richmond], Whig, Aug. 15, 1834, 1
Davis, Mrs. Sarah, Bedford, Whig, March 26, 1824, 3
Davis, Thomas E., New Kent, Whig, March 8, 1838, 2
Davis, Wm., Sr., Lynchburg, Whig, Sept. 7, 1829, 3
Dawson, Benj. A., Richmond, Enquirer, Jan. 16, 1808, 3
Dawson, Mrs. Philadelphia, Richmond, Enquirer, Sept. 12, 1807, 3
Day, Maj. Benjamin, Fredericksburg, Enquirer, Feb. 24, 1821, 3
Day, Mrs. Lucy, Richmond, Whig, April 22, 1820, 3
Day, Samuel, Hanover, Enquirer, Feb. 5, 1811, 3
Delear, James, Chesterfield, Enquirer, May 12, 1808, 3
Demoville, Peter, Charles City, Whig, June 30, 1835, 3
Demoville, Capt. Samuel, Charles City, Enquirer, Sept. 28, 1813, 3
Denegre, John M., Southampton, Whig, April 21, 1837, 2
Denegre, John, Southampton, Whig, Dec. 20, 1836, 3
Denhom, Maj. Archibald, Richmond, Enquirer, July 12, 1815, 3
Dennie, Mrs. Richmond, Enquirer, July 8, 1817, 3
Denoon, Daniel, Richmond, Enquirer, March 2, 1826, 3
Denson, Mrs. Ann, Richmond, Whig, Oct. 17, 1831, 1
Depriest, Mrs. Jane Eliza, Marion Hill, Whig, Feb. 16, 1836, 3
DeSear, Chesterfield, Enquirer, May 12, 1808, 3
Devine, Owen, Richmond, Whig, May 8, 1835, 3
Dewson, George Baldwin, Richmond, Whig, Oct. 10, 1834, 4
Dickenson, Fountaine C., Albemarle, Enquirer, Oct. 29, 1813, 3
Dickenson, Mrs. Sally, Richmond, Enquqirer, July 20, 1816, 3
Dickinson, A. G., Chilesburg, Enquirer, Dec. 1, 1826, 3
Dickinson, Robert, Nottoway, Enquirer, Jan. 23, 1819, 3
Dickinson, Thomas, Caroline, Enquirer, July 25, 1826, 3
Dickinson, Thomas T., Caroline, Whig, Feb. 11, 1825, 3; Enquirer, May
    17, 1825, 3
Dickinson, William, Caroline, Enquirer, Oct. 7, 1823, 3
Digges, Col. Cole, Hanover, Enquirer, March 4, 1817, 3
Digges, Margaretta E., Richmond, Whig, Oct. 28, 1830, 3
Digges, Mrs. Mary R., Hanover, Enquirer, Feb. 14, 1826, 3

Dillon, Edward D., Prince Edward, Enquirer, Nov. 6, 1818, 3
Dinkens, Mrs. ————, Enquirer, Oct. 4, 1822, 3
Dixon, Capt. John, Richmond, Enquirer, May 24, 1805, 3
Dixon, Mary E., Williamsburg, Whig, Feb. 23, 1836, 1
Dobie, Thomas, Petersburg, Whig, June 15, 1830, 2
Doddridge, Hon. Philip, ————, Whig, Nov. 23, 1832, 1
Dolton, Mrs. Eliza, Chesterfield, Enquirer, Oct. 21, 1817, 3
Donnison, Joseph, Tappahannock, Enquirer, May 14, 1808, 3
Dorlon, Capt. John, Nansemond, Enquirer, June 4, 1824, 3
Dorman, Mrs. Amanda, Lexington, Whig, Oct. 5, 1829, 2
Dorsett, Mrs. Elizabeth, Richmond, Whig, April 22, 1830, 3
Doswell, Dr. Benjamin Franklin, Caroline, Whig, Nov. 1, 1828, 3
Doswell, Capt. James, Hanover, Enquirer, July 8, 1825, 3
Doswell, James M., Forks of Hanover, Enquirer, Sept. 10, 1819, 3
Douglas, Brig. Gen. Hugh, Loudoun, Enquirer, July 12, 1815, 3
Douglass, William, New Kent, Enquirer, Jan. 31, 1826, 3
Douthat, Robert, Charles City, Whig, May 21, 1828, 3; Enquirer, May 23, 1828, 3
Douthat, Wm., Westover, Whig, Sept. 23, 1829, 3
Downing, John, Louisa, Whig, Aug. 21, 1832, 1
Downing, Col. Thomas T., Northumberland, Enquirer, May 18, 1816, 4
Downman, James W. P., Lancaster, Whig, Nov. 4, 1834, 1
Doyle, David, Hanover, Enquirer, Sept. 3, 1814, 3
Doyle, David, Richmond, Enquirer, Feb. 6, 1817, 3
Doyle, John, Richmond, Whig, April 1, 1829, 3
Drake, Elizabeth Adelaide, Powhatan, Whig, May 17, 1836, 2
Drake, Mary Powhatan, Enquirer, Jan. 24, 1828, 3
Drake, William, Powhatan, Whig, April 18, 1837, 2
Draper, Maj. Samuel C., Wythe, Enquirer, Sept. 20, 1825, 3
Drew, Carter H., Richmond, Enquirer, Sept. 21, 1819, 3
Drewry, Henry, Sussex, Whig, Oct. 4, 1828, 3; Enquirer, Oct. 21, 1828, 3
Drewry, John, Petersburg, Whig, May 9, 1837, 2
Driscoll, Asa, Manchester, Whig, Sept. 25, 1829, 3
Drummond, John, York, Enquirer, Jan. 15, 1824, 3
Drummond, Capt. Richard, Norfolk, Whig, Nov. 29, 1836, 2
Drumwright, Lucas, Mecklenburg, Whig, April 15, 1831, 1
Dudley, Mrs. Ann H., King William, Enquirer, Oct. 8, 1824, 3
Dudley, Baylor, Surry, Enquirer, Feb. 13, 1827, 3
Dudley, Peter A., New Kent, Whig, April 14, 1835, 3
Duke, Wm. Burnley, Hanover, Whig, Aug. 26, 1834, 3
Dulany, Mrs. Frances A. C., Shuter's Hill, Whig, May 12, 1835, 3
Duncan, Capt. Wm., King William, Whig, Oct. 21, 1836, 1
Dunlop, James, Petersburg, Enquirer, July 20, 1827, 3
Dunlop, Nathaniel, Fluvanna, Whig, July 24, 1838, 2
Dunn, Mrs. Mary E., Botetourt, Enquirer, June 22, 1827, 3
Dunton, Maj. Wm., Northampton, Whig, June 19, 1835, 1
Dupree, Benjamin, Greensville, Enquirer, Feb. 15, 1811, 3
Dupuy, James, Nottoway, Enquirer, Aug. 15, 1823, 3
Dupuy, Peter, Richmond, Whig, Sept. 1, 1826, 3; Enquirer, Sept. 1, 1826, 3

Durphie, Francis, Charles City, Whig, March 23, 1829, 3
Duval, Benj., Lynchburg, Whig, July 28, 1826, 2
Dyball, Henry, Richmond, Whig, July 19, 1828, 3
Dykes, James, Norfolk, Enquirer, Oct. 5, 1819, 3

E.

Eanes, Mary Booker, Amelia, Enquirer, Nov. 28, 1823, 3
Edgar, Capt. Thomas, Bedford, Whig, Dec. 2, 1825, 1
Edmonds, Mrs. Adelaide, Fauquier, Whig, Oct. 6, 1837, 4
Edmondson, Joseph, Hanover, Enquirer, April 16, 1819, 3
Edmondson, Capt. Robert, Washington, Enquirer, Feb. 15, 1823, 3
Edmondson, Samuel, Jr., —————, Enquirer, Dec. 29, 1826, 3
Edmondson, Col. William, Washington, Enquirer, Aug. 30, 1822, 3
Edmund, Harrison, Amelia, Enquirer, July 18, 1820, 3
Edwards, Mrs. Eleanor, King William, Enquirer, Oct. 21, 1825, 3
Edwards, Mrs. Elizabeth, King William, Whig, Jan. 9, 1828, 3
Edwards, James B., King William, Whig, Sept. 19, 1834, 2
Egan, Dr. John Bradshaw, Powhatan, Enquirer, July 19, 1825, 3
Ege, Mrs. Elizabeth, Richmond, Whig, Jan. 10, 1829, 3
Ege, Samuel H., Richmond, Enquirer, Sept. 13, 1815, 3
Eggleston, Mrs. Ann C., Hanover, Enquirer, Aug. 10, 1816, 3
Eggleston, Edmund, Hanover, Enquirer, Dec. 23, 1809, 3
Eggleston, Edward, Amelia, Whig, Nov. 11, 1836, 2
Eggleston, Maj. Joseph, Amelia, Enquirer, Feb. 22, 1811, 3; Feb. 26, 1811, 4
Eggleston, Mrs. Maria, Cumberland, Enquirer, Jan. 31, 1824, 3
Eggleston, Mrs. Martha, Amelia, Enquirer, Dec. 6, 1821, 3
Eggleston, Mrs. Matilda, Amelia, Enquirer, Dec. 6, 1821, 3
Eggleston, Susan A. E., Louisa, Whig, July 12, 1833, 1
Eisenminger, Lewis, Portsmouth, Whig, Jan. 31, 1833, 3
Elcan, Marcus, Richmond, Enquirer, May 12, 1808, 3
Eldridge, Bartlett, —————, Whig, Sept. 29, 1826, 3
Eldridge, Mrs. Susannah, Buckingham, Enquirer, April 10, 1821, 3
Eleves, Mrs. Adelaide, Norfolk, Enquirer, Nov. 22, 1825, 3
Ellett, Lemuel Balor, Richmond, Whig, Nov. 4, 1836, 3
Ellett, Mrs. Mary, Goochland, Whig, March 23, 1830, 3
Ellett, Mrs. Sarah, King William, Whig, Jan. 9, 1828, 3
Ellicott, Andrew, West Point, Enquirer, Sept. 8, 1820, 3
Ellicott, John, Richmond, Enquirer, June 25, 1811, 3
Ellicott, Mary, Richmond, Enquirer, July 22, 1806, 3
Ellicott, Thomas, —————, Enquirer, July 30, 1811, 3
Ellis, Mrs. Elizabeth, Hanover, Whig, Jan. 20, 1826, 3
Ellis, Col. John Amherst, Enquirer, Feb. 16, 1826, 3
Ellis, John, Amherst, Enquirer, Aug. 29, 1823, 3
Ellis, Thomas H., [formerly of Amherst County], Enquirer, Sept. 19, 1804, 3
Ellis, Thomas H., Amherst, Enquirer, Jan. 17, 1824, 3
Ellyson, Richard, Richmond, Whig, Nov. 28, 1837, 4

Ellzey, Col. William, Loudoun, Whig, Dec. 8, 1835, 4
Eppes, John T., King William, Whig, Nov. 11, 1834, 4
Eppes, Gen. Richard, Sussex, Whig, Aug. 7, 1832, 3
Estes, Mrs. Jane C., Nelson, Whig, Sept. 26, 1837, 2
Epperson, John, Buckingham, Enquirer, July 8, 1806, 3
Eppes, John W., —————, Enquirer, Sept. 19, 1823, 3
Eskridge, Gerard B., Staunton, Enquirer, Sept. 6, 1822, 3
Eskridge, Sally G., Staunton, Enquirer, Aug. 17, 1821, 3
Eustace, Hancock, Stafford, Whig, Aug. 5, 1829, 3
Eustace, James Henry, Stafford, Enquirer, Jan. 9, 1821, 3
Eustace, Mrs. Martha, Richmond, Enquirer, May 23, 1828, 3
Eustace, Mrs. Martha J., Richmond, Whig, May 21, 1828, 3
Eustace, William, Stafford, Whig, Aug. 16, 1825, 3; Enquirer, Aug. 16, 1825, 3
Evans, Mrs. Elizabeth, Richmond, Whig, Nov. 3, 1831, 3
Evans, George, Chesterfield, Enquirer, July 5, 1822, 3
Evans, John, Columbia, Enquirer, Nov. 21, 1823, 3
Evans, Mrs. Mary, King William, Enquirer, Oct. 29, 1819, 3
Evans, Mrs. Mary E., Cartersville, Whig, Set. 12, 1834, 3
Evans, Mrs. Sarah W., King and Queen, Whig, June 28, 1833, 2
Evans, Thos. R., King William, Whig, March 26, 1824, 3
Evans, Wm. Thomas, Richmond, Enquirer, April 29, 1828, 3
Everett, Mrs. Elizabeth P., Richmond, Whig, Nov. 11, 1834, 2
Exall, Lucy B., Richmond, Whig, July 23, 1833, 3

F.

Farley, Arthur, Powhatan, Whig, Nov. 30, 1832, 3
Farley, Mrs. Frances, Nottoway, Whig, April 13, 1838, 2
Farley, Washington, Powhatan, Whig, Nov. 30, 1832, 3
Farrar, Christopher, Richmond, Whig, Aug. 13, 1833, 2
Farrar, Nimrod, Richmond, Whig, June, 17, 1830, 3
Faulcon, Nicholas, Mount Pleasant, Enquirer, April 14, 1826, 3
Faulcon, Nicholas, Surry, Enquirer, April 7, 14, 1826, 3
Fauntleroy, Mrs. Isabella, Middlesex, Enquirer, Sept. 24, 1819, 3
Fauntleroy, John, Middlesex, Enquirer, Oct. 5, 1824, 3
Fauntleroy, Samuel G., King and Queen, Enquirer, Dec. 23, 1826, 3
Fenwick, Wm., Richmond, Whig, Feb. 7, 1829, 2
Ferguson, Elizabeth, Buckingham, Enquirer, Aug. 20, 1813, 4
Ferguson, John, —————, Enquirer, Oct. 8, 1824, 3
Field, Dr. Richard, Brunswick, Whig, May 27, 1829, 3
Field, Mrs. Susan, Petersburg, Enquirer, Oct. 4, 1805, 3
Field, Theophilus, Brunswick, Enquirer, Aug. 1, 1826, 3
Finch, Wm. H., Surry, Enquirer, Feb. 3, 1827, 3
Finley, Mrs. Mary, Augusta, Whig, Oct. 15, 1829, 3
Finnell, George, Culpeper, Enquirer, Aug. 20, 1819, 3
Finney, Capt. Wm., Powhatan, Whig, Dec. 29, 1835, 3
Fisher, Alexander B., Richmond, Enquirer, Nov. 8, 1815, 3
Fisher, Mrs. Anne, Richmond, Whig, June 29, 1832, 3

Fisher, Mrs. Elizabeth, Richmond, Whig, May, 21, 1833, 2
Fisher, John A. B., Richmond, Enquirer, Nov. 11, 1815, 3
Fitzgerald, Robert, Cumberland, Enquirer, April 8, 1815, 3
Fitzhugh, John, Stafford, Enquirer, May 19, 1809, 3
Fitzhugh, Mrs. Mary, Williamsburg, Enquirer, Oct. 25, 1822, 3
Fitzhugh, W., Prince William, Whig, Nov. 15, 1836, 2
Fitzhugh, Wm. H., Fairfax, Whig, May 26, 1830, 2
Fitzwhylsonn, Mrs. Sarah, Richmond, Enquirer, March 11, 1808, 3
Fitzwhylson, William H., Richmond, Whig, June 23, 1837, 1
Fitzwilson, Mrs. Fanny, Richmond, Whig, Sept. 12, 1831, 4
Fleisher, Casper, Richmond, Enquirer, Dec. 7, 1811, 3
Fleisher, Mrs. Hannah, Richmond, Whig, May 13, 1830, 3
Fleming, Mrs. Lucy Eleanor, Goochland, Whig, Sept. 24, 1824, 3; Enquirer, Sept. 2, 1824, 3
Fleming, William, Chesterfield, Whig, Feb. 20, 1824, 3; Enquirer, Feb. 19, 21, 1824, 3
Fleshman, Sarah, Charlotte, Whig, Oct. 5, 1829, 2
Flood, Maj. Henry, Buckingham, Enquirer, July 24, 1827, 3
Flood, James, Norfolk, Enquirer, June 10, 1815, 3
Flood, Capt. John, Buckingham, Whig, Sept. 5, 1826, 3; Enquirer, Aug. 22, 1826, 3
Flood, Mrs. Nancy P., Jefferson, Whig, Nov. 16, 1832, 4
Floyd, Correlly, Montgomery, Whig, July 23, 1833, 3
Folkes, Rev. Edward, Charles City, Enquirer, Sept. 24, 1824, 3
Fontaine, Edmund Overton, Buckingham, Whig, Dec. 9, 1836, 4
Fontaine, Maria, Richmond, Whig, July 19, 1836, 3
Fontaine, Wm. R., Hanover, Enquirer, June 22, 1824, 3
Forbes, John, Richmond, Whig, March 28, 1834, 1
Ford, Gertrude, Lynchburg, Whig, July 3, 1838, 4
Ford, John C., Chesterfield, Whig, Sept. 28, 1832, 1
Ford, Pascal, Cumberland, Enquirer, March 4, 14, 1826, 3
Ford, Rev. Reuben, Hanover, Enquirer, Oct. 14, 1823, 3
Ford, Col. Samuel, Amelia, Enquirer, Aug. 13, 1824, 3
Ford, William, Richmond, Whig, Dec. 4, 1835, 2
Ford, Capt. William, Stafford, Whig, Sept. 19, 1834, 2
Forsce, William, Chesterfield, Enquirer, May 2, 1817, 3
Foster, John, Richmond, Whig, March 15, 1825, 3
Foster, Mary, Richmond, Enquirer, Dec. 26, 1809, 3
Fountleroy, Mrs. Isabella, Middlesex, Enquirer, Sept. 24, 1819, 3
Fountleroy, John, Middlesex, Enquirer, Oct. 5, 1824, 3
Fountleroy, Samuel G., King and Queen, Enquirer, Dec. 23, 1826, 3
Foushee, John H., Richmond, Enquirer, Nov. 17, 1812, 3
Foushee, Mrs. Lucy, Richmond, Enquirer, Nov. 4, 1814, 3
Foushee, Dr. William, Sr., Richmond, Whig, Aug. 27, 1824, 3; Enquirer, Aug. 24, 1824, 3
Fowler, Luke, Charles City, Enquirer, Sept. 27, 1822, 3
Fowler, William, Richmond, Whig, June 8, 1838, 2
Fox, Capt. John, King William, Enquirer, Jan. 7, 1815, 3
Francisco, Peter, Richmond, Whig, Jan. 17, 1831, 3

Franklin, Mrs. Elizabeth, Richmond, Whig, Oct. 9, 1832, 3
Franklin, George, Henrico, Whig, Oct. 28, 1834, 4
Franklin, Capt. Robert, Norfolk, Enquirer, Aug. 27, 1813, 3
Frayser, Beverly, Richmond, Whig, Sept. 2, 1834, 1
Frayser, Mrs. Elizabeth, Cumberland, Whig, Sept. 12, 1837, 4
Frayser, Jackson, Henrico, Enquirer, March 30, 1821, 3
Frayser, Lucy, Henrico, Whig, Nov. 8, 1825, 3
Frayser, Lucy Frances, Richmond, Whig, Sept. 16, 1834, 2
Frayser, Mrs. Philip, Henrico, Whig, Jan. 20, 1837, 2
Frazer, Alexander, Richmond, Enquirer, Oct. 13, 1809, 3
Freeman, Col. Constant, Washington, Enquirer, March 4, 1824, 3
Freeman, Mrs. Samuel [Sarah], ————, Whig, April 21, 1837, 2
French, Ansel, Richmond, Whig, Sept. 25, 1832, 1
French, Maj. David, Giles, Whig, Oct. 24, 1833, 3
French, Mrs. Elizabeth, Hampton, Enquirer, March 22, 1815, 3
French, Dr. George, Fredericksburg, Enquirer, June 11, 1824, 3
French, Dr. Stephen L., Warrenton, Enquirer, Aug. 24, 1827, 3
French, Wm., Prince William, Enquirer, May 30, 1826, 3
Friend, Mrs. Alfred, Manchester, Whig, Oct. 20, 1835, 3
Friend, Mrs. Frances W. Cabell, Richmond, Whig, July 31, 1838, 4
Frosser, William, Henrico, Enquirer, June 22, 1824, 3
Fuller, Bartholomew, Staunton, Enquirer, Aug. 15, 1823, 3
Fulton, Alexander, Henrico, Enquirer, Sept. 9, 1823, 3

G.

Gaines, Mrs. Elizabeth, King and Queen, Whig, March 17, 1837,
Gaines, Thomas Muse, Richmond, Enquirer, June 30, 1818, 3
Gains, Mrs. Martha, Albemarle, Enquirer, May 4, 1824, 2
Gairdner, Gorge, Richmond, Enquirer, March 12, 1805, 3
Gallagher, James, Dumfries, Enquirer, April 18, 1826, 3
Gallaher, James, Jefferson, Whig, May 30, 1837, 2
Galligo, Joseph, Richmond, Enquirer, July 3, 1818, 3
Galt, Mrs. Elizabeth, Williamsburg, Enquirer, Nov. 15, 1822, 3
Galt, John E., Richmond, Enquirer, Feb. 6, 1813, 3
Galt, Mrs. Rosanna, Richmond, Whig, April 26, 1828, 3
Galt, William, Richmond, Enquirer, March 9, 1825, 3; April 1, 1825, 3
Galt, William T., Williamsburg, Whig, Aug. 8, 1826, 3
Gamble, Mrs. Catharine, Richmond, Whig, Jan. 3, 1832, 1
Gamble, Mrs. Charlotte S., Richmond, Enquirer, Nov. 3, 1809, 3
Gamble, Col. Robert, Richmond, Enquirer, April 13, 27, 1810, 3
Gardiner, George, ————, Enquirer, March 12, 1805, 3
Gardiner, John, Richmond, Whig, Nov. 3, 1826, 3
Gardner, Ann Hubbard, Richmond, Whig, Nov. 30, 1830, 3
Gardner, Dr. Anthony, King and Queen, Enquirer, Oct. 4, 1819, 3
Gardner, Mrs. Elizabeth, King and Queen, Enquirer, Oct. 19, 1824, 3
Gardner, Elizabeth Hunter, Henrico, Whig, Oct. 10, 1837, 2
Gardner, Lavinia M., Louisa, Enquirer, Sept. 24, 1824, 3
Gardner, Maj. Thomas, Louisa, Whig, April 26, 1836, 3

Gardner, William, Hanover, Enquirer, Nov. 23, 1819, 3
Garland, Benj. N., Richmond, Enquirer, March 24, 1812, 3
Garland, Edward, Goochland, Enquirer, Sept. 24, 1822, 3
Garland, Mrs. Maria, Richmond, Whig, May 27, 1831, 4
Garland, Mrs. Mary C., Mecklenburg, Whig, July 8, 1834, 4
Garlick, Robert P., King William, Whig, June 8, 1838, 2
Garner, Olivia C., Tappahannock, Whig, July 15, 1834, 1
Garnett, Mrs. Ann, King and Queen, Enquirer, July 25, 1828, 3
Garnett, Mrs. Ann Maria, King and Queen, Enquirer, July 11, 1828, 3
Garnett, Mrs. James M. [Mary E. D.], Essex, Whig, April 21, 1837, 1
Garnett, James M., Jr., Essex, Enquirer, July 27, 1824, 3
Garnett, Muscoe, Essex, Enquirer, March 24, 1807, 3
Garnett, Nancy, Essex, Whig, Oct. 20, 1835, 4
Garnett, Reuben, Caroline, Enquirer, Aug. 26, 1825, 3
Garnett, Robert C., Richmond, Whig, Aug. 20, 1833, 4
Garnett, Mrs. Sarah Henrietta, Whig, Dec. 29, 1837, 2
Garraur, Mrs. Mary, Richmond, Whig, Jan. 20, 1837, 2; Jan. 24, 1837, 4
Garrett, Robert Winder, Williamsburg, Whig, Jan. 9, 1838, 2
Garrett, Mrs. Sarah, King and Queen, Enquirer, June 18, 1824, 3
Garrett, William, Essex, Enquirer, July 29, 1825, 3
Garrison, George B., Belfield, Whig, Dec. 5, 1827, 3
Garrow, William, Warwick, Enquirer, Jan. 13, 1816, 3
Garthright, Mrs. Martha, Goochland, Whig, Feb. 9, 1836, 3
Garthright, Samuel, Jr., Richmond, Whig, Oct. 3, 1831, 4
Gary, Elizabeth, Richmond, Whig, March 15, 1831, 3
Gatewood, Chany, King and Queen, Enquirer, Nov. 27, 1821, 3
Gatewood, Mrs. Mary, Essex, Whig, Oct. 30, 1832, 2
Gatewood, Philip, King and Queen, Whig, Sept. 30, 1829, 3
Gatliff, Susan, Williamsburg, Enquirer, Oct. 22, 1822, 3; Enquirer, Nov. 12, 1822, 3
Gautier, Mrs. Frances, Richmond, Enquirer, Aug. 5, 1806, 3
Gay, Mrs. Judith, Goochland, Whig, Nov. 4, 1827, 3
Gay, Wm., Richmond, Whig, Oct. 6, 1831, 3
Geddy, Mrs. Ann, New Kent, Enquirer, Nov. 7, 1823, 3
Gee, Mrs. Eliza, Lunenburg, Enquirer, April 23, 1819, 3
Gentry, Mrs. Hannah, Richmond, Enquirer, May 21, 1811, 3
Gentry, Mrs. Sarah W., Richmond, Whig, Oct. 2, 1835, 2
George, Rev. Enoch, Staunton, Whig, Sept. 3, 1828, 3; Enquirer, Sept. 5, 1828, 3
Gerow, Maj. James, King and Queen, Enquirer, Jan. 22, 1822, 3
Gholson, Mrs. Ann Jane, Cumberland, Whig, Dec. 30, 1831, 2
Ghoslon, Maj. Wm., Brunswick, Whig, April 12, 1831, 3
Gibb, Catharine Virginia, Richmond, Whig, Aug. 10, 1832, 3
Gibb, James, Richmond, Whig, May 25, 1832, 3
Gibbon, Mrs. Ann, Richmond, Enquirer, Dec. 2, 1823, 3
Gibbons, John Nicholson, Norfolk, Whig, May 16, 1837, 2
Gibbons, William D., Frederick, Whig, Dec. 16, 1837, 4
Gibbs, Dr. John C., Halifax, Enquirer, Feb. 14, 1824, 3
Gibson, Patrick, Richmond, Enquirer, Dec. 20, 1827, 3

Gifford, Mrs. Fortune, Whig, April 27, 1830, 3
Gildart, Mrs. Eleanor, Richmond, Whig, April 23, 1824, 3
Giles, Abraham B. Venable, ——————, Enquirer, Jan. 2, 1817, 3
Giles, Edmund, M., Petersburg, Whig, May 8, 11, 1838, 1
Giles, Mrs. Francis Ann, Amelia, Enquirer, Jan. 3, 1822, 3
Giles, Kennon, Chesterfield, Whig, Aug. 10, 1830, 3
Giles, Mrs. William B., ——————, Enquirer, Aug. 23, 1808, 3
Gill, Mary Virginia, Richmond, Whig, Sept. 10, 1833, 2
Gilliam, Carter, Richmond, Whig, Jan. 25, 1833, 4
Gilliam, Carter N., Mount Erin, Whig, Dec. 15, 1834, 1
Gilliam, Dr. James S., Petersburg, Enquirer, April 13, 1814, 3
Gilliam, James S., Petersburg, Enquirer, June 16, 1820, 3
Gilmer, Francis W., Charlottesville, Enquirer, Feb. 28, 1826, 3; Whig, Feb. 28, 1826, 3
Gilmer, Peachy R., Albemarle, Whig, April 15, 1836, 4
Gilmour, Wm., Lancaster, Whig, July 21, 1826, 3; Enquirer, Aug. 11, 1826, 3
Gipson, Miles, Buckingham, Enquirer, April 15, 1823, 3
Glenn, Mrs. Francis T., Gloucester, Enquirer, Feb. 28, 1828, 3
Glenn, Parke, Richmond, Enquirer, Nov. 10, 1820, 3
Glenn, Mrs. Susanna, Richmond, Whig, Dec. 14, 1830, 3
Goddin, Albert, Richmond, Enquirer, Oct. 22, 1822, 3
Goddin, Mrs. Amanda, Richmond, Whig, Dec. 19, 1829, 3
Goddin, Avery, New Kent, Enquirer, Sept. 3, 1822, 3
Goddin, John, James City, Enquirer, Sept. 27, 1825, 3; Whig, Sept. 20, 1825, 3
Goddin, Loftin Clay, near Richmond, Whig, Sept. 30, 1834, 3
Godfrey, Ann D., Richmond, Enquirer, Oct. 18, 1808, 3
Godwin, W. C., Nansemond, Whig, June 19, 1835, 1
Goff, Capt. Wm., Manchester, Whig, Sept. 28, 1832, 3
Goggin, Mrs. Mary C., Richmond, Whig, March 20, 1835, 1
Goggin, Col. Pleasant M., Bedford, Whig, Feb. 11, March 28, 1831, 3
Gooch, Mrs. Sally, Amherst, Enquirer, Nov. 15, 1822, 3
Gooch, William B., Amherst, Enquirer, Aug. 31, 1816, 3
Goodall, Mrs. Martha Burwell, ——————, Enquirer, Sept. 27, 1822, 3
Goodall, Parke, Hanover, Enquirer, Jan. 11, 1816, 3
Goode, Bennet, Powhatan, Enquirer, March 23, 1821, 3
Goode, Francis, Powhatan, Enquirer, May 7, 1814, 3
Goode, Mrs. Martha H., Powhatan, Enquirer, July 19, 1825, 3
Goode, Col. Samuel, Mecklenburg, Enquirer, Dec. 3, 1822, 3
Goode, Mrs. Sarah B., Mecklenburg, Enquirer, July 15, 1825, 3
Goode, Theoderick, Chesterfield, Enquirer, May 8, 1810, 3
Goodnow, William, Richmond, Whig, Oct. 6, 1831, 4
Goodrich, John, Isle of Wight, Enquirer, June 14, 1808, 3
Goodrich, Meshack, Surry, Enquirer, Dec. 11, 1823, 3
Goodwin, Mrs. Elizabeth K., Louisa, Whig, Dec. 22, 1830, 3
Goodwin, Reuben, Hanover, Enquirer, June 22, 1813, 3
Goodwin, Capt. William, ——————, Enquirer, June 19, 1816, 3
Goodwyn, John, Lunenburg, Whig, Jan. 13, 1837, 3

Goodwyn, Col. Peterson, ————, Enquirer, Feb. 26, 1818, 3
Goodwyn, Uriah G., [formerly of Richmond], Whig, Sept. 30, 1830, 3
Goran, Mrs. Elizabeth, King and Queen, Enquirer, Oct. 22, 1822, 3
Gordon, Daniel, [formerly of Manchester], Enquirer, Jan. 21, 1813, 3
Gordon, Mrs. Elizabeth, King and Queen, Enquirer, Oct. 22, 1822, 3
Gordon, James, Botetourt, ————, Enquirer, June 24, 1825, 3
Gordon, Mrs. Janetta, Richmond, Enquirer, Feb. 24, 1821, 3
Gordon, Richard H., James City, Enquirer, Nov. 14, 21, 1826, 3
Gordon, William, Northumberland, Whig, June 5, 1827, 3
Gorhan, Richard H., James City, Enquirer, Nov. 21, 1816, 3
Goss, Wm. W., Albemarle, Whig, Aug. 28, 1838, 2
Gouldman, Mrs. Judith, Buckingham, Whig, March 8, 1836, 3
Graeme, Robert, Richmond, Whig, May 26, 1830, 3
Graham, Mrs. Eliza, Manchester, Enquirer, June 11, 1819, 3
Graham, John, Richmond, Enquirer, Sept. 26, 1820, 3
Graham, Robert, Prince William, Enquirer, July 6, 1821, 3
Grant, Mrs. Charity, Richmond, Whig, Sept. 16, 1836, 3
Grant, James, Richmond, Enquirer, Dec. 3, 1822, 3
Grant, Mrs. Mary, Chesterfield, Whig, March 14, 1830, 3
Grantland, Mrs. Ann, ————, Enquirer, Dec. 30, 1823, 3
Grantland, Mrs. Christiana, Richmond, Whig, Aug. 11, 1831, 4
Grantland, John, Richmond, Enquirer, Feb. 10, 1824, 3
Grantland, Michael, Waynesboro, Enquirer, Aug. 8, 1820, 3
Grantland, Capt. Samuel, Hanover, Enquirer, Aug. 10, 1824, 3
Grantland, Mrs. Samuel, Hanover, Enquirer, Aug. 10, 1824, 3
Granville, Smith, Goochland, Whig, Jan. 10, 1826, 3
Graves, John, Jr., Louisa, Whig, Jan. 17, 1837, 1
Graves, Rachael Angelina, Richmond, Whig, Aug. 21, 1832, 3; Whig,
    Aug. 24, 1832, 1
Graves, Col. Richard, New Kent, Whig, April 7, 1835, 4
Graves, Sally Henry Rebecca, Sussex, Whig, Oct. 3, 1831, 4
Graves, Sarah C., Chesterfield, Whig, Aug. 26, 1836, 2
Graves, Maj. Thomas, Chesterfield, Whig, Sept. 5, 1837, 1
Graves, Mrs. Virginia Bolling, ————, Whig, Jan. 28, 1836, 3
Gray, Alfred Wherry, Richmond, Whig, March 12, 1829, 3
Gray, Francis, Lynchburg, Enquirer, June 1, 1827, 3
Gray, Gurden, Richmond, Whig, Oct. 17, 1831, 2
Gray, John, Monroe, Enquirer, Jan. 3, 1821, 3
Gray, John C., Southampton, Enquirer, May 27, 1823, 3
Gray, Mrs. Phebe, Goochland, Enquirer, Oct. 14, 1808, 3
Gray, William, Sr., Prince Edward, Enquirer, June 27, 1826, 3
Greaner, Catherine Jane, Richmond, Whig, May 4, 1831, 3
Green, Archibald, Mecklenburg, Enquirer, Nov. 28, 1826, 3
Green, Mrs. Elizabeth Aubin, Amelia, Enquirer, Nov. 23, 1819, 3
Green, Mrs. Elizabeth, Orange, Enquirer, May 13, 1825, 3
Green, Mrs. Ellen, Culpeper, Whig, Aug. 4, 1831, 4
Green, John, Culpeper, Enquirer, Oct. 29, 1819, 3
Green, John W., Richmond, Enquirer, May 13, 1823, 3
Green, Louisa M., Mecklenburg, Enquirer, July 26, 1825, 3

Green, Mrs. Margaret F., Culpeper, Whig, Dec. 24, 1831, 3
Green, Mrs. Mary, Westmoreland, Enquirer, July 19, 1825, 3
Green, Richard P., Hanover, Whig, Nov. 16, 1829, 3
Green, Thomas, [formerly of Fredericksburg], Enquirer, Nov. 23, 1821, 3
Greenaway, Robert, Dinwiddie, Whig, Dec. 5, 1837, 2
Greene, Richard, Richmond, Whig, Oct. 5, 1832, 1
Greenhow, Dr. James, Richmond, Enquirer, Dec. 30, 1815, 3
Greenhow, Samuel, Richmond, Enquirer, Feb. 18, 1815, 3
Greenlow, Mrs. Mary, —————, Enquirer, July 19, 1825, 3
Greenway, Elizabeth Kennon, Dinwiddie, Whig, March 13, 1838, 3
Gregory, James, Richmond, Whig, Nov. 4, 1825, 3
Gregory, Joannes, Jefferson, —————, Enquirer, Nov. 18, 25, 1823, 3
Gregory, John F., James City, Enquirer, April 20, 1827, 3
Gregory, Mary Ann Sutherland, King William, Enquirer, Oct. 4, 1825, 3
Gregory, William A., Fredericksburg, Enquirer, April 4, 1820, 3
Grey, John C., Southampton, Enquirer, May 27, 1823, 3
Griffin, Judge Cyrus, —————, Enquirer, Dec. 18, 1810, 3
Griffin, Obediah, Henrico, Whig, Oct. 10, 1834, 4
Griffin, Richard, Richmond, Whig, Aug. 29, 1834, 3
Griffin, Thomas B., Yorktown, Whig, Oct. 14, 1836, 4
Griffith, Mrs. Elizabeth, Henrico, Whig, Aug. 15, 1826, 3
Griffith, Mrs. Martha, Richmond, Whig, April 11, 1834, 1
Grimes, Martha, West End, Enquirer, May 13, 1822, 4
Grimes, Mary, West End, Enquirer, Aug. 13, 1822, 4
Grimes, Philip, West End, Enquirer, Aug. 13, 1822, 4
Grimsly, Martha Ann, Richmond, Whig, July 21, 1837, 2
Groom, Richard, Fluvanna, Enquirer, Jan. 4, 1827, 3
Grover, Benjamin, Richmond, Enquirer, May 4, 1816, 3
Grubbs, Matthew, Louisa, Enquirer, Dec. 28, 1820, 3
Grymes, Mrs. Judith, Middlesex, Enquirer, Oct. 30, 1816, 3
Grymes, Dr. Robert N., King George, Whig, Dec. 19, 1837, 4
Grymes, Mrs. Sarah, Orange, Whig, July 17, 1832, 1
Guerrant, Mrs. Caroline Elizabeth, Goochland, Enquirer, Aug. 22, 1828, 3
Guerrant, Capt. Daniel, Buckingham, Enquirer, Feb. 25, 1826, 3
Guerrant, Robert P., Goochland, Enquirer, July 26, 1808, 3
Guigon, A. E., Richmond, Whig, Feb. 5, 1833, 3
Guigon, Mrs. Marian, Richmond, Whig, Dec. 30, 1831, 1
Guigon, Mary Amelia, Richmond, Enquirer, July 15, 1828, 3; Whig, July 19, 1828, 3
Gunn, Mrs. Ann Eliza, New Kent, Enquirer, Sept. 10, 1819, 3
Gustin, Robert, Morgan, Whig, March 30, 1838, 2
Guy, Mrs. Ann, Caroline, Enquirer, Sept. 27, 1815, 3
Guy, George M., Richmond, Whig, April 15, 1830, 3
Guy, Mrs. Mahettable J. W., Henrico, Whig, Feb. 25, 1836, 1
Guy, Mrs. Mary, Augusta, Whig, May 24, 1830, 2
Guy, Mrs. Mary, Caroline, Enquirer, June 29, 1819, 3
Guy, William, Caroline, Enquirer, March 17, 1807, 3
Gwathmey, Mrs. Ann Maria, Richmond, Enquirer, Oct. 4, 1819, 3
Gwathmey, Maj. Joseph, King William, Enquirer, Feb. 19, 1824, 3

Gwathmey, Joseph H., Richmond, Enquirer, March 4, 1824, 3
Gwathmey, Mrs. Margaret, Richmond, Enquirer, Aug. 10, 1824, 3
Gwathmey, Mrs. Richard [Ann], King William, Whig, April 21, 1837, 2
Gwathmey, Temple, King and Queen, Whig, March 26, 1831, 1
Gwyn, Caroline F., Gloucester, Enquirer, June 17, 1828, 3

H.

Hackett, Agnes, Louisa, Enquirer, July 1, 1828, 3
Hackett, Thomas Terrell, Louisa, Enquirer, Jan. 19, 1826, 3
Haden, Capt. Joseph, Fluvanna, Enquirer, Nov. 10, 1820, 3
Hagan, Michael, Richmond, Whig, March 16, 1824, 3
Haile, John, Tappahannock, Enquirer, Dec. 31, 1818, 3
Hales, Mrs. Mary B., Buckingham, Whig, Aug. 28, 1830, 3
Haley, John L., Richmond, Whig, Jan. 28, 1831, 3
Hall, Frederic, Suffolk, Enquirer, Oct. 24, 1823, 3
Hall, Margaret, Gloucester, Enquirer, Nov. 5, 1817, 3
Hallam, Edward, Richmond, Whig, Oct. 31, 1831, 2
Hallam, Giles, Richmond, Whig, March 8, 1836, 3
Hallam, Nicholas, White Sulphur, Enquirer, Aug. 31, 1816, 3
Hallyburton, Mrs. James D. [Ann C.], New Kent, Whig, Feb. 24, 1837, 4
Hallyburton, Patrick, Richmond, Whig, June 15, 1833, 1
Hamersley, Mary A., Fairfax, Whig, Sept. 4, 1832, 1
Hamilton, Giles, Richmond, Whig, Feb. 21, 1837, 3
Hammond, Nathan, —————, Enquirer, July 22, 1825, 3
Hancock, Col. George, —————, Enquirer, Aug. 8, 1820, 3
Hancock, William, Manchester, Whig, May 1, 1835, 3
Hankins, William, York, Whig, March 17, 1837, 4
Hannor, Capt. John, Halifax, Enquirer, Jan. 17, 1826, 3
Hardgrove, Mary Frances, Richmond, Whig, Jan. 6, 1837, 2
Hardie, Mrs. Sophia A., Richmond, Whig, Jan. 30, 1829, 2
Hardin, Mahala, Powhatan, Enquirer, Sept. 22, 1820, 3
Hardin, Gen. Martin Davis, —————, Enquirer, Oct. 28, 1823, 3
Harding, George, Powhatan, Enquirer, Sept. 24, 1822, 3
Harding, Mrs. Hannah, Northumberland, Whig, Jan. 23, 1827, 3
Harding, John B., Powhatan, Enquirer, Oct. 12, 1821, 3
Harding, Peter Giles, Amelia, Whig, Aug. 26, 1825, 3; Enquirer, Aug.
    16, 1825, 3
Harding, Thomas Perkins, Louisa, Whig, Oct. 16, 1832, 1
Hardon, Mrs. Nancy, Manchester, Enquirer, Feb. 22, 1827, 3
Hardy, Mrs. Janet, Richmond, Whig, Dec. 30, 1829, 3
Hardy, Mrs. Sarah H., Richmond, Whig, Oct. 31, 1837, 2
Hargrove, Wm., Rocketts, Whig, Oct. 26, 1832, 1
Hargrove, Wm. K., King William, Whig, Oct. 5, 1829, 2
Hariston, Col. Geo., Henry, Enquirer, April 10, 1822, 3
Harper, Wm. [formerly of Virginia], Enquirer, Feb. 14, 1822, 3
Harris, Mrs. Caroline Matilda, Powhatan, Whig, Dec. 23, 1825, 3
Harris, Mrs. Caroline S., Richmond, Whig, Nov. 14, 1831, 3
Harris, Caroline S., Richmond, Whig, Oct. 9, 1832, 1

Harris, Mrs. Charles T., Halifax, Enquirer, Feb. 26, 1822, 3
Harris, Maj. John, Chesterfield, Enquirer, Dec. 21, 1815, 3
Harris, Mrs. Margaret, Chesterfield, Whig, Feb. 2, 1831, 3
Harris, Mrs. Margaret, Chesterfield, Enquirer, March 15, 1825, 3
Harris, Mrs. Margaret Lucinda, Spotsylvania, Whig, Sept. 26, 1827, 3;
Enquirer, Oct. 2, 1827, 3
Harris, Mrs. Mary, Albemarle, Enquirer, Feb. 4, 1819, 3
Harris, Mrs. Mary, Nelson, Enquirer, April 11, 1828, 3
Harris, Mrs. Mildred W., Powhatan, Enquirer, Oct. 31, 1828, 3
Harris, Mrs. Sally G., Powhatan, Whig, Jan. 3, 1831, 3
Harris, Mrs. Sarah, Richmond, Enquirer, Nov. 28, 1817, 3
Harris, William L., Hanover, Enquirer, March 11, 1817, 3
Harriss, Francis, Buckingham, Enquirer, July 17, 1827, 3
Harrison, Mrs. Ann [formerly of Lynchburg], Whig, March 20, 1832, 1
Harrison, Braxton, Charles City, Enquirer, May 16, 1809, 3
Harrison, Carter B., Maycox on James River, Enquirer, April 19, 1808, 3
Harrison, Edmund, Amelia, Whig, Feb. 7, 1826, 3; Enquirer, Feb. 7,
1826, 3
Harrison, Mrs. Edmund [Martha W.], Amelia, Whig, April 18, 1837, 4
Harrison, Mrs. Jacob, Richmond, Enquirer, Nov. 5, 1805, 3
Harrison, Jacob, Richmond, Enquirer, May 20, 1817, 3
Harrison, John Cleves Simmes, North Bend, Whig, Nov. 12, 1830, 3
Harrison, Mrs. Judith Page, Caroline, Whig, July 25, 1834, 1
Harrison, Mrs. Martha, Manchester, Whig, Sept. 15, 1831, 3
Harrison, Mrs. Martha, Richmond, Whig, May 14, 1830, 3
Harrison, Mrs. Martha W., Amelia, Whig, April 18, 1837, 4
Harrison, Mrs. Mary, Cumberland, Whig, Oct. 20, 1835, 4
Harrison, Matthew, Dumfries, Enquirer, Sept. 12, 1807, 3
Harrison, Polly, Richmond, Enquirer, June 11, 1819, 3
Harrison, Mrs. Rebecca C., Charles City, Whig, Dec. 11, 1832, 1
Harrison, Thos. R., Goochland, Whig, Nov. 5, 1833, 2
Harrison, Virginia, Richmond, Whig, Dec. 14, 1830, 3
Hart, Martin, Charlotte Court House, Whig, March 31, 1835, 3
Harvey, Capt. J. D., Charlotte, Whig, May 31, 1825, 3
Harvie, Edwin James, Richmond, Enquirer, Jan. 4, 18, 1812, 3
Harvie, Col. John, near Richmond, Enquirer, Feb. 13, 1807, 3
Harvie, Lewis, Richmond, Enquirer, April 21, 1807, 3
Harvie, Mrs. Margaret, Richmond, Whig, Dec. 2, 1825, 3; Enquirer, Dec.
2, 1825, 3
Harvey, Capt. J. D., Charlotte, Enquirer, June 3, 1825, 3
Harvey, Col. Matthew, Botetourt, Enquirer, Oct. 21, 1823, 3
Harwood, Col. Archibald R., King and Queen, Whig, Sept. 26, 1837, 4
Harwood, Capt. Daniel P., Henrico, Whig, Nov. 1, 1833, 1
Haskins, Mrs. Ann B., Powhatan, Whig, Sept. 29, 1837, 2
Haskins, John H., Chesterfield, Whig, March 24, 1838, 4
Haskins, Capt. Robert, Chesterfield, Enquirer, April 25, 1826, 3
Haskins, Thomas B., Powhatan, Whig, May 15, 1835, 4
Hatcher, Mrs. Catharine, Bedford, Whig, Aug. 22, 1834, 1
Hatcher, Mrs. Elizabeth, Cumberland, Whig, Nov. 6, 1830, 3

Hatcher, Dr. Hardaway, Powhatan, Enquirer, Nov. 5, 1819, 3
Hatcher, John, Cumberland, Whig, Aug. 15, 1837, 4
Hatcher, Maj. John, Cumberland, Enquirer, Jan. 31, 1826, 3
Hatchett, Dr. Archibald, Lunenburg, Enquirer, Sept. 1, 1820, 3
Hawkins, Mrs. Elizabeth, Richmond, Enquirer, March 23, 1816, 3
Hawkins, James Oscar, Richmond, Whig, Jan. 20, 1837, 2
Hawkins, John, Richmond, Whig, Dec. 30, 1831, 1
Hawkins, Capt. Robert, Chesterfield, Enquirer, April 25, 1826, 3
Hawkins, Mary, Brookville, Whig, Sept. 21, 1829, 3
Haxall, Philip, Richmond, Whig, Dec. 30, 1831, 1
Haxall, Wm., Petersburg, Whig, July 25, 1834, 1
Hay, Charles, ————————, Whig, April 26, 1833, 1
Hay, Hon. Geo., Eastern Shore, Whig, Sept. 23, 1830, 3
Hay, Mrs. Rebecca, Richmond, Enquirer, March 24, 1807, 3
Hayes, Mrs. Ann Dent, Richmond, Whig, Nov. 14, 1831, 3
Hayes, Dr. John, Richmond, Whig, Oct. 28, 1834, 4
Hay, James, ————————, Enquirer, Oct. 10, 1804, 3
Hays, Silas, Richmond, Whig, June 22, 1832, 3
Hays, Slowey, Richmond, Whig, Oct. 21, 1836, 1
Hays, Thomas P., Henrico, Enquirer, Oct. 7, 1808, 3
Haywood, John, Davidson, Enquirer, Jan. 18, 1827, 3
Hazard, Capt. George R., Richmond, Whig, March 12, 1833, 3
Head, John, Wythe Court House, Whig, Nov. 15, 1833, 2
Heath, Henry C., Henrico, Enquirer, Oct. 9, 1816, 3
Heath, Hon. John, ————————, Enquirer, Oct. 16, 1810, 3
Heath, Mrs. Maria C., Richmond, Whig, Sept. 12, 1834, 4
Heffernan, Rev. Henry, Middlesex, Enquirer, March 12, 1814, 3
Heiskell, Maj. Adam, Hampshire, Enquirer, May 13, 1822, 4
Heiskell, John, Winchester, Whig, Dec. 9, 1836, 4
Heiskell, Mrs. Margaret, Staunton, Whig, May 30, 1837, 2
Hemingway, Benjamin, Richmond, Whig, Jan. 12, 1830, 3
Henderson, Dabney, Fredericksburg, Whig, Dec. 28, 1824, 3
Henderson, Mrs. Frances S., Richmond, Whig, Feb. 14, 1831, 3
Henderson, Mrs. Harriet Jane, Richmond, Whig, Feb. 13, 1828, 3
Henderson, James, Nottoway, Enquirer, Nov. 18, 1817, 3
Henderson, John W., Richmond, Whig, May 5, 1831, 2
Henderson, Mrs. Maria, Richmond, Whig, June 14, 1832, 3
Henderson, Richard O., Manchester, Whig, Nov. 1, 1828, 3
Hendree, George, Portsmouth, Whig, July 11, 1834, 4
Hendren, Mrs. Alice, Charles City, Enquirer, Nov. 21, 1820, 3
Hendren, Alice Eaton, Petersburg, Enquirer, Nov. 7, 1823, 3
Hening, Mrs. Agatha, Richmond, Whig, April 12, 1828, 3; Enquirer,
    April 13, 1828, 3
Hening, William Waller, Richmond, Enquirer, April 4, 1828, 3; Whig,
    April 5, 12, 1828, 3
Henley, Leonard, Williamsburg, Whig, Feb. 9, 1831, 3
Henley, Martha, Smithfield, Enquirer, Sept. 24, 1811, 3
Henley, Mrs. Mary Ann, Henrico, Enquirer, Dec. 20, 1814, 3
Henly, Mrs. Polly, Amelia, Enquirer, April 26, 1815, 3

Henry, Mrs. Ann, Charlotte, Enquirer, May 12, 1808, 3
Henry, Mrs. Caroline Matilda, Spottsylvania, Whig, Sept. 26, 1837, 4
Henry, James, Northumberland, Enquirer, Jan. 18, 1805, 3
Henry, Mary, Stafford, Enquirer, Aug. 14, 1821, 3
Henshaw, Edward, Richmond, Whig, July 3, 1832, 1
Henshaw, Mary Ann, Berkley, Whig, Feb. 23, 1836, 3
Herbert, Jane, Alexander, Enquirer, Sept. 2, 1825, 3
Herbert, Noblet, Alexander, Enquirer, Sept. 2, 1825, 3
Herbert, Robert, Alexander, Enquirer, Sept. 2, 1825, 3
Hereford, Mrs. Elizabeth, Prince William, Whig, Nov. 17, 1837, 4
Hereford, John W., Fairfax, Whig, Oct. 5, 1832, 1
Hereford, Mrs. Mary, Mason, Whig, Nov. 3, 1831, 4
Herndon, Wm. Albert, Spottsylvania, Whig, Aug. 9, 1828, 3
Heron, John E., [formerly of Richmond], Whig, Feb. 28, 1832, 4
Herring, Stephenson Daniel, Rockingham, Whig, June 29, 1838, 1
Heth, Maj. Harry, Chesterfield, Enquirer, March 3, 1821, 3
Heth, Henry, Black Heath, Enquirer, Feb. 7, 1824, 3
Heth, Capt. John, Richmond, Enquirer, Nov. 20, 1810, 3
Heywood, Nathaniel M., Richmond, Whig, Oct. 26, 1832, 1
Hichok, Mrs. Hannah, Scottsville, Whig, Jan. 31, 1832, 3
Hickman, William, Powhatan, Enquirer, Nov. 21, 24, 1820, 3
Hickman, Wm. P., King William, Whig, Aug. 26, 1825, 3
Hicks, Mrs. Edward [Elizabeth], Brunswick, Whig, Feb. 17, 1837, 3
Hicks, Edwin G., Brunswick, Whig, June 13, 1837, 2
Hickson, Mrs. Mary, Richmond, Whig, July 25, 1834, 2
Higginbotham, David, Albemarle, Enquirer, March 4, 1823, 3
Higginbotham, Mrs. Francis, Amherst, Enquirer, June 28, 1825, 3
Higginbotham, John, Nelson, Enquirer, March 19, 1822, 3
Hill, Mrs. Ann, Spottsylvania, Enquirer, Aug. 3, 1827, 3
Hill, Brooke, King and Queen, Whig, Oct. 31, 1834, 2
Hill, Edward, King and Queen, Enquirer, Jan. 23, 1816, 3
Hill, Mrs. Eliza C., Hanover, Enquirer, March 4, 1815, 3
Hill, Elizabeth D., Caroline, Whig, Nov. 17, 1835, 4
Hill, Mrs. Emily Brooke, King William, Whig, Aug. 15, 1834, 1
Hill, Francis, Greenville, Enquirer, Nov. 22, 1805, 3
Hill, George, [native of Virginia], Whig, May 22, 1838, 1
Hill, Hannah M., Caroline, Enquirer, Oct. 8, 1824, 3
Hill, Hetty A., King William, Whig, Oct. 31, 1834, 1
Hill, Mrs. Isaac, —————, Enquirer, July 27, 1824, 3
Hill, James, Amelia, Enquirer, June 24, 1825, 3
Hill, James Myrvin, New Kent, Whig, March 29, 1831, 1
Hill, John, New Kent, Enquirer, Sept. 3, 1822, 3
Hill, Mrs. Judith B., King William, Whig, Oct. 18, 1833, 1
Hill, Robert, King William, Enquirer, Jan. 1, 1814, 3
Hill, Capt. Robert B., King and Queen, Whig, July 15, 1834, 3
Hillard, Henry, Richmond, Whig, July 29, 1834, 1
Hillyard, Mrs. Mariah, King William, Enquirer, Aug. 30, 1822, 3
Hillyard, Mary N., Richmond, Enquirer, Jan. 15, 1822, 3
Hinton, Mrs. Anstis, Richmond, Whig, May 23, 1834, 1

Hinton, James S., Richmond, Whig, Aug. 15, 1834, 2
Hipkins, Capt. Leroy, —————, Enquirer, Oct. 14, 1808, 3
Hite, Maj. Isaac, Frederick, Whig, Dec. 9, 1836, 4
Hite, Maj. Robert G., Charleston, Enquirer, Sept. 23, 1823, 3
Hocker, Mrs. Ann, Buckingham, Enquirer, July 19, 1825, 3; Whig, July 15, 1825, 3
Hodgsen, Wm. P., Petersburg, Enquirer, June 29, 1813, 3
Hodgson, Ann, Fluvanna, Whig, Feb. 2, 1838, 2
Hoge, Rev. John Blair, Berkley, Enquirer, April 11, 1826, 3
Hoge, Rev. Moses, Prince Edward, Enquirer, July 11, 1820, 3
Holcombe, Philemon H. W., Amelia, Enquirer, July 25, 1823, 3
Holladay, Capt. James, Spottsylvania, Enquirer, March 4, 1823, 3
Holladay, Capt. Lewis, Spottsylvania, Enquirer, March 4, 1823, 3
Holladay, Lewis, Spottsylvania, Enquirer, Nov. 3, 1820, 3
Holland, Mrs. Mary, Cumberland, Enquirer, July 20, 1819, 3
Holloway, Maj. David, Richmond, Enquirer, Oct. 21, 1823, 3
Holloway, Mrs. L. H., Richmond, Enquirer, Nov. 28, 1826, 3
Holman, Mrs. Ann, Cumberland, Whig, Feb. 28, 1833, 1
Holman, Joseph George, Long Island, Enquirer, Sept. 2, 1817, 3
Holmes, David, Winchester, Whig, Aug. 31, 1832, 4
Holmes, Mrs. Elizabeth, Frederick, Enquirer, Sept. 8, 1826, 3
Holmes, Hugh, Winchester, Whig, Feb. 11, 1825, 3; Enquirer, Feb. 1, 1825, 3
Holt, Mrs. Ann M., Hanover, Enquirer, Aug. 30, 1825, 3
Holt, Henry, Richmond, Enquirer, Feb. 16, 1813, 3
Holt, John E., Norfolk, Whig, Oct. 16, 1832, 3
Holtz, Mrs. Elizabeth, Richmond, Enquirer, Dec. 11, 1813, 3
Holyburton, Dr. William, New Kent, Whig, Nov. 29, 1825, 2
Holyoke, Dr. Edward Augustus, Salem, Whig, April 6, 1829, 3
Home, Henrietta, Richmond, Whig, Aug. 14, 1832, 1
Honyman, Dr. Robert, Hanover, Enquirer, May 6, 1824, 2
Hood, Thomas, Manchester, Whig, April 12, 1828, 3; Enquirer, April 15, 1828, 3
Hooe, Arthur Edward, King George, Whig, June 17, 1836, 3
Hooe, John, Fauquier, Enquirer, Oct. 22, 1819, 3
Hooe, Mrs. Maria M. G., Prince William, Whig, Sept. 23, 1834, 4
Hooe, William F., Fairfax, Enquirer, July 7, 1826, 4
Hooe, Wm. Fitzhugh, King George, Whig, Aug. 23, 1833, 2
Hooker, Mrs. Ann, Buckingham, Whig, July 15, 1825, 3
Hoomes, Mrs. Anne C., Caroline, Enquirer, March 27, 1810, 3
Hoomes, Col. Armistead, Bowling Green, Enquirer, Feb. 6, 1827, 3; Whig, Feb. 6, 1827, 3
Hoomes, Maj. John, Caroline, Enquirer, March 23, 1824, 3
Hoomes, Capt. John, Bowling Green, Enquirer, Dec. 27, 1805, 3
Hoomes, Mrs. Judith, Bowling Green, Enquirer, Aug. 16, 1822, 3
Hoomes, Mrs. Lucy Mary, Caroline, Enquirer, Aug. 13, 1814, 3
Hoomes, Thomas C., King and Queen, Enquirer, Feb. 10, 1821, 3
Hoones, Richard, Bowling Green, Enquirer, Dec. 27, 1823, 3
Hooper, Mrs. Agnes, Richmond, Whig, May 30, 1834, 1

Hooper, Benjamin T., ——————, Enquirer, Feb. 16, 1826, 3
Hooper, Lion E., Buckingham, Whig, Aug. 25, 1837, 2
Hopkins, Armistead S., Richmond, Whig, May 14, 1830, 3
Hopkins, John, Winchester, Enquirer, Oct. 30, 1827, 3
Hopkins, John S., New Kent, Whig, April 20, 1831, 4
Horsley, Col. John, Buckingham, Enquirer, Dec. 5, 1828, 3
Horsley, Thomas Jefferson, Richmond, Whig, June 29, 1838, 1
Horwell, Julia, Richmond, Whig, Dec. 27, 1836, 2
Hoskins, Two Children, King and Queen, Enquirer, Nov. 22, 1825, 3
Hoskins, Mrs., King and Queen, Enquirer, Nov. 22, 1825, 3
Hoskins, Catharine M., King and Queen, Whig, June 1, 1838, 2
Hoskins, John, King and Queen, Enquirer, Nov. 26, 1813, 3
Hoskins, Polly, King and Queen, Enquirer, Nov. 22, 1825, 3
Hotchkiss, Josiah, Caroline, Whig, Sept. 7, 1832, 1
Howard, Mrs. Eliza, Richmond, Whig, Oct. 4, 1836, 3
Howard, Col. John Enger, Richmond, Enquirer, Oct. 16, 1824, 3
Howard, Thomas C., Richmond, Whig, Sept. 9, 1834, 2
Howe, Dr. Jonas, ——————, Enquirer, July 22, 1825, 3
Howell, Giles Hamilton, Richmond, Whig, Feb. 21, 1837, 3
Howell, John F., Norfolk, Enquirer, Sept. 14, 1821, 3
Howle, Mrs. Ann, New Kent, Enquirer, June 9, 1826, 3
Howlett, Alexander, Richmond, Whig, April 10, 1838, 1
Hubard, Louisana, Buckingham, Whig, Oct. 26, 1832, 2
Hubbard, Amos L., Richmond, Whig, Jan. 14, 1831, 1
Hubbard, James T., Richmond, Enquirer, Sept. 18, 1812, 3
Hubbard, John K., Charles City, Enquirer, Sept. 10, 1819, 3
Hubbard, Dr. Thomas, Surrey, Enquirer, Sept. 14, 1827, 3
Hubuer, John C., Richmond, Enquirer, Dec. 28, 1813, 3
Hudgins, Mrs. Ann, Mathews, Enquirer, Dec. 6, 1823, 3
Hudgins, William G., Gloucester, Whig, Aug. 13, 1830, 3
Hudson, Barrett Price, Charlotte, Enquirer, April 1, 1828, 3
Hudson, Christopher E., Chesterfield, Enquirer, Dec. 23, 1823, 3
Hudson, Elizabeth L., Charlotte, Whig, Dec. 5, 1827, 3; Enquirer, Dec. 4, 1827, 3
Hudson, Francis E., City Point, Enquirer, Oct. 9, 1827, 3
Hudson, James Turner, Chesterfield, Whig, March 16, 1831, 3
Hudson, Mrs. Martha, Prince Edward, Enquirer, April 2, 1822, 3
Hughes, Leander, Richmond, Enquirer, April 13, 1813, 3
Hughes, Mrs. Margaret J., Patrick, Enquirer, Sept. 24, 1819, 3
Hughes, Mary, Patrick, Enquirer, Nov. 16, 1827, 3
Hughes, Mrs. Susan, Fluvanna, Whig, Jan. 31, 1837, 4
Hull, Mrs. Harriet W., Richmond, Whig, March 10, 1836, 3
Hume, Humphrey, Culpeper, Whig, Feb. 27, 1838, 1
Humes, Louisa, Belle Isle, Enquirer, May 19, 1826, 3
Humes, Mrs. Margaret, Smyth, Whig, Feb. 21, 1835, 3
Hungerford, Matilda E., Richmond, Whig, April 14, 1835, 3
Hunnicutt, Samuel B., Prince George, Whig, May 8, 1838, 1
Hunt, Mrs. Catherine, Richmond, Whig, Jan. 6, 1832, 3
Hunt, David [native of Virginia], Whig, March 29, 1828, 3

Hunt, George, Lynchburg, Whig, Oct. 17, 1829, 3
Hunter, Mrs. Antoinette, near Wythe Court House, Whig, May 22, 1835, 2
Hunter, Capt. Archibald, Montgomery, Enquirer, Oct. 25, 1822, 3
Hunter, David, Berkeley, Enquirer, Dec. 21, 1813, 3
Hunter, Mrs. Elizabeth, Richmond, Enquirer, Dec. 22, 1825, 3
Hunter, Col. Henry, ————, Enquirer, Nov. 12, 1822, 3
Hunter, James, Essex, Enquirer, Feb. 28, 1826, 3
Hunter, Muscoe Garnet, Williamsburg, Enquirer, July 4, 1817, 3
Hunton, Gen. Thomas, Fauquier, Enquirer, Nov. 7, 1826, 3
Hurley, Edward, [formerly of Richmond], Enquirer, Sept. 9, 1823, 3
Hurt, Polly W., Halifax, Enquirer, Dec. 21, 1815, 3
Hutchison, Capt. Daniel C., Richmond, Whig, Jan. 19, 1832, 1
Hutton, George, Henrico, Whig, April 17, 1834, 1
Hutton, Gen. Thos., Fauquier, Whig, Nov. 3, 1826, 3
Hyde, Capt. Robt, Richmond, Whig, Dec. 15, 1835, 1
Hylton, Daniel L., ————, Enquirer, Jan. 22, 24, 1811, 3

I.

Irby, Eliza Jane, Nottoway, Enquirer, Nov. 3, 1826, 3
Irvin, Crawford, Richmond, Whig, Nov. 4, 1829, 3
Irving, Dr. Charles R., Amelia, Whig, April 28, 1835, 4
Irving, Mrs. Elizabeth H., Cartersville, Whig, Aug. 26, 1836, 2
Irving, Robert, Cartersville, Whig, Feb. 20, 1838, 1
Isbell, Joseph, Louisa, Enquirer, Aug. 1, 1823, 3
Ives, George, Richmond, Whig, Oct. 31, 1831, 4
Izard, Mrs. Elizabeth Carter, [formerly of Virginia], Enquirer, July 21, 1826, 3

J.

Jackson, Maj. Charles, Louisa, Enquirer, Dec. 20, 1823, 3
Jackson, Edward B., Clarksburg, Whig, Oct. 3, 1826, 3
Jackson, Dr. Edward B., Clarksburg, Enquirer, Sept. 29, 1826, 3
Jackson, Ephraim, Brunswick, Enquirer, Sept. 6, 1825, 3
Jackson, John G., Clarksburg, Whig, April 12, 1825, 3; Enquirer, April 12, 15, 1825, 3
Jackson, Mrs. Lucy, Richmond, Whig, Oct. 14, 1830, 3
Jackson, Mrs. Margaret, Richmond, Whig, July 3, 1832, 1
Jackson, Mary Jane, Richmond, Whig, Aug. 5, 1836, 1
Jacobs, Joseph, Richmond, Enquirer, Jan. 4, 1812, 3
Jacobs, Solomon, Richmond, Enquirer, Nov. 6, 1827, 3
James, Alfred, Hanover, Enquirer, Sept. 9, 1823, 3
James, Mrs. Eliza Matilda, Louisa, Enquirer, Dec. 2, 1825, 3
James, Ellen Maria, Richmond, Enquirer, Nov. 11, 1825, 3
James, Fleming, Richmond, Whig, Oct. 14, 1825, 3
James, Mrs. Frances R., Richmond, Whig, March 16, 1831, 3
James, Lucy Temple, Richmond, Whig, April 23, 1831, 3
James, Maria Terrell, Richmond, Enquirer, Sept. 16, 1823, 3

James, Rebecca Minor, Richmond, Enquirer, Sept. 23, 1828, 3
James, Mrs. Susannah, Hanover, Whig, May 31, 1833, 1
James, Mrs. William, Cumberland, Enquirer, Aug. 24, 1819, 3
Janey, Alexander, Essex, Enquirer, Sept. 6, 1825, 3
Janney, Mrs. Elizabeth, Henrico, Whig, March 20, 1832, 1
Jefferson, Martha, Lunenburg, Enquirer, Oct. 21, 1823, 3
Jefferson, Thomas, Albemarle, Enquirer, July 7, 1826, 2; Whig, July 7, 1826, 2
Jeffress, Margaret B., Charlotte, Enquirer, June 12, 1827, 3
Jeffries, Thomas, Lunenburg, Enquirer, May 31, 1822, 3
Jenkins, Mrs. Mary, Norfolk, Enquirer, Aug. 28, 1821, 3
Jenkins, Mary Ann, Richmond, Whig, Jan. 27, 1826, 3
Jenkins, Mary B., Orange, Enquirer, Oct. 12, 1821, 3
Jenkins, Thomas, Orange, Enquirer, Dec. 15, 1821, 3
Jenkins, Uriah, Manchester, Whig, Jan. 13, 1837, 3
Jennings, James O., Cartersville, Whig, Sept. 9, 1834, 3
Jennings, Lucy, James City, Whig, Sept. 9, 1836, 4
Jennings, Capt. Robert, Charlotte, Enquirer, Nov. 7, 1806, 3
Jennings, Sally Ann, Cartersville, Enquirer, Dec. 22, 1827, 3; Jan. 3, 1828, 3
Jennings, Capt. Thomas, Norfolk, Whig, Oct. 9, 1832, 3
Jerdone, Francis, New Kent, Whig, May 10, 1836, 2
Jerdone, James, New Kent, Whig, Sept. 16, 1836, 3
Jerdone, James, Louisa, Enquirer, Whig, Aug. 3, 1827, 3
Johnson, Mrs. Ann C. H., Louisa, Enquirer, April 28, 1820, 3
Johnson, Bailey S., Hanover, Whig, July 14, 1830, 3
Johnson, Hon. C. C., ————, Whig, June 22, 1832, 1
Johnson, David, Richmond, Enquirer, June 27, 1823, 3
Johnson, Francis, Fluvanna, Whig, March 30, 1838, 2
Johnson, James, Isle of Wight, Enquirer, Dec. 13, 1325, 3
Johnson, James, Norfolk, Enquirer, Dec. 13, 1825, 3
Johnson, Mrs. Jane, King William, Whig, Dec. 11, 1835, 3
Johnson, John, Fluvanna, Enquirer, April 23, 1819, 3
Johnson, Capt. John, Wythe, Whig, Jan. 25, 1830, 3
Johnson, John I., ————, Whig, July 23, 1828, 3
Johnson, Dr. Littleton J., Accomac, Whig, Jan. 26, 1838, 4
Johnson, Mrs. Lucy, King William, Whig, April 11, 1826, 3
Johnson, Lucy Beverly, Richmond, Whig, Oct. 28, 1834, 4
Johnson, Mrs. Mary, ————, Enquirer, Sept. 28, 1819, 3
Johnson, Mildred M., Louisa, Enquirer, Sept. 4, 1816, 3
Johnston, Ann Blackburn, Richmond, Whig, Jan. 3, 1832, 3
Johnson, Mrs. Miranda, King William, Whig, Nov. 13, 1832, 3
Johnston, Charles, Botetourt, Whig, Feb. 5, 1833, 3
Johnston, James M., Richmond, Whig, July 9, 1833, 3
Johnston, John, Gloucester, Enquirer, April 6, 1827, 3
Johnston, Mrs. Mary, Abingdon, Enquirer, July 1, 1825, 3
Johnston, Mrs. Sarah W., Richmond, Enquirer, June 17, 1823, 3
Johnston, William, Louisa, Enquirer, Dec. 20, 1814, 3
Jones, Abner, Richmond, Whig, Jan. 28, 1825, 3

Jones, Mrs. Angelica, Richmond, Whig, Nov. 18, 1836, 2
Jones, Mrs. Ann, Surry, Whig, Aug. 1, 1837, 1
Jones, Mrs. Ann, Richmond, Enquirer, Jan. 24, 1811, 3
Jones, Bathurst, Hanover, Enquirer, April 6, 1810, 3
Jones, Berthur, Richmond, Whig, June 9, 1837, 2
Jones, Chamberlayne, Amelia, Whig, June 10, 1829, 3
Jones, Maj. Churchill, Orange, Enquirer, Sept. 24, 1822, 3
Jones, Daniel, Sr., James City, Enquirer, Dec. 24, 1822, 3
Jones, David, Cumberland, Whig, April 4, 1829, 3
Jones, Mrs. Elizabeth R., Hanover, Enquirer, June 6, 1826, 3
Jones, Gabriel, Rockingham, Enquirer, Oct. 31, 1806, 3
Jones, Harrison, Richmond, Whig, Aug. 29, 1829, 3
Jones, Jane Clark, Richmond, Whig, Aug. 15, 1834, 1
Jones, Jekyll, Richmond, Enquirer, Aug. 2, 1815, 3
Jones, Capt. John, Fluvanna, Enquirer, June 3, 1828, 3
Jones, John, Warwick, Enquirer, Feb. 3, 1824, 3
Jones, John Abner, Hanover, Whig, Nov. 24, 1835, 2
Jones, John M., Lynchburg, Whig, Jan. 7, 1830, 3
Jones, John R., Richmond, Enquirer, Sept. 21, 1819, 3; Sept. 28, 1819, 3
Jones, John W., Gloucester, Whig, May 19, 1835, 1
Jones, John Waller, Westmoreland, Enquirer, May 13, 1825, 3
Jones, Hon. Joseph, Richmond, Enquirer, Nov. 5, 1805, 3
Jones, Gen. Joseph, Petersburg, Enquirer, Feb. 12, 1824, 3
Jones, Leanner Calpernia, Richmond, Whig, Aug. 17, 1832, 3
Jones, Leopold, Richmond, Whig, Sept. 7, 1829, 3
Jones, Levi, Mansfield, Enquirer, Aug. 27, 1813, 2
Jones, Lewis Sommers, Richmond, Whig, Oct. 16, 1832, 3
Jones, Mrs. Margaret, Rockingham, Enquirer, Oct. 25, 1822, 3
Jones, Mrs. Mary, Fluvanna, Enquirer, April 13, 1827, 3
Jones, Mrs. Mary, Gloucester, Enquirer, May 19, 1820, 3
Jones, Mary Elizabeth, Albemarle, Whig, Dec. 27, 1837, 4
Jones, Meriwether, ————, Enquirer, Aug. 19, 22, 1806, 3
Jones, Mrs. Paulina, Henrico, Enquirer, Oct. 29, 1819, 3
Jones, Peter, Isle of Wight, Whig, March 17, 1829, 3
Jones, Robert K., Petersburg, Enquirer, Aug. 27, 1824, 3
Jones, Skelton, Richmond, Enquirer, Oct. 30, 1812, 3
Jones, Mrs. Susanna S., Nottoway, Enquirer, Nov. 18, 1823, 3
Jones, Dr. Walter, Northumberland, Enquirer, Feb. 13, 1816, 3
Jones, William, Fredericksburg, Enquirer, July 20, 1816, 3
Jones, Dr. William P., ————, Enquirer, June 29, 1819, 3
Jones, Capt. Williamson P., Lancaster, Whig, July 4, 1837, 2
Jordon, Mrs. Elizabeth T., Buckingham, Whig, March 17, 1837, 2
Jordon, Robert, Suffolk, Enquirer, Jan. 27, 1824, 3
Jordon, Taverner, Botetourt, Enquirer, July 31, 1821, 3
Jouett, Maj. John, Bath, Enquirer, March 26, 1822, 3
Judah, Bareech H., Richmond, Whig, Sept. 27, 1830, 2
Jude, Frederick, Richmond, Whig, Sept. 30, 1836, 2
Jude, John H., Spring Grove, Whig, March 11, 1825, 3

K.

Kean, Andrew, Goochland, Whig, Dec. 5, 1837, 2
Kean, Mrs. Caroline M., Caroline, Whig, Sept. 22, 1831, 1
Kearnes, Nevin, Richmond, Enquirer, Dec. 24, 1816, 3
Keatts, Mrs. Martha, Lunenburg, Whig, Sept. 6, 1828, 3
Keesee, Charles, —————, Enquirer, Feb. 20, 1817, 3
Keesee, Griffin, Henrico, Enquirer, May 11, 1821, 3
Keesee, Nancy Sharp, Henrico, Whig, April 15, 1836, 4
Kelly, George, Norfolk, Enquirer, April 28, 1920, 3
Kemp, Mrs. Hannah, Richmond, Enquirer, March 30, 1827, 3
Kemp, Matthew S., Gloucester, Whig, Aug. 9, 1828, 3
Kemp, Peter, Gloucester, Enquirer, Dec. 30, 1809, 3
Kemp, Peter, Middlesex, Enquirer, Aug. 13, 1819, 3
Kendall, Mrs. Margaret, Richmond, Enquirer, March 11, 1826, 3
Kennedy, James F., Alexandria, Enquirer, June 15, 1813, 3
Kennedy, Robert, Richmond, Whig, March 16, 1830, 3
Kennon, Beverly Randolph, Powhatan, Whig, April 7, 1837, 4
Kennon, Elizabeth D., Norfolk, Whig, Sept. 28, 1832, 1
Kennon, Nancy, Powhatan, Whig, April 7, 1837, 4
Kerr, Mrs. Elizabeth, Richmond, Whig, Nov. 4, 1834, 1
Kerr, Mrs. Elizabeth, Powhatan, Whig, April 26, 1834, 3
Key, John R., Richmond, Whig, May 26, 1837, 2
Key, Sandy, Fluvanna, Whig, Aug. 3, 1838, 1
Kidd, William Campbell, Richmond, Whig, Sept. 2, 1825, 3; Enquirer, Sept. 2, 1825, 3
Kie, Mrs. Mary Christian, Fluvanna, Enquirer, Nov. 13, 1821, 3
Kilby, John Thompson, Nansemond, Whig, June 19, 1838, 4
Kimbrough, Joseph, Richmond, Whig, Sept. 8, 1829, 3
Kimbrough, Dr. William, Louisa, Enquirer, Jan. 30, 1808, 3
King, Mrs. Harriet, Hanover, Whig, Dec. 16, 1836, 4,
King, William, Abingdon, Enquirer, Nov. 8, 1808, 3
Kirby, Mrs. Eliza Ann, Brunswick, Whig, July 4, 1837, 2
Kirke, John, —————, Enquirer, March 20, 1810, 3
Knauff, Mrs. Ann S. C., Farmville, Whig, April 29, 1836, 1
Knight, Mrs. Martha, Lunenburg, Whig, Nov. 9, 1824, 3
Knowls, Mrs. Margaret, Richmond, Whig, Jan. 20, 1837, 4
Knox, Eliza Whittle, Mecklenburg, Enquirer, May 6, 1828, 3
Krauth, John M., Richmond, Whig, Dec. 28, 1824, 3
Kyle, Wm., Fincastle, Whig, July 3, 1832, 3

L.

Labby, Mrs. Mary, [formerly of Richmond], Whig, March 8, 1836, 1
Lackland, Capt. John, Cumberland, Enquirer, May 16, 1809, 3
Lackland, Mrs. Mary, Richmond, Enquirer, Oct. 20, 1820, 3
Lackland, Zadock, Buckingham, Enquirer, April 13, 1827, 3
Lacy, Charles H., Richmond, Whig, Oct. 1, 1833, 2

Ladd, Oliver, Charles City, Whig, Nov. 6, 1832, 2
Ladd, Sarah, Charles City, Enquirer, March 12, 1814, 3
Ladd, Thomas, Nansemond, Whig, May 27, 1834, 4
Lafon, Rev. Thomas, Chesterfield, Enquirer, Oct. 2, 1816, 3
Lakenan, Elizabeth P., Richmond, Enquirer, July 31, 1812, 3
Lamb, Richard, Norfolk, Whig, Jan. 18, 1833, 1
Lamb, Mrs. Sarah, Richmond, Whig, April 6, 1831, 3
Lambert, George, Bedford, Whig, March 10, 1837, 4
Lambert, Mrs. William [Mary Ann], Richmond, Whig, March 10, 1837, 2
Land, Jeremiah T., Princess Anne, Whig, March 16, 1832, 4
Lane, Col. John, Amelia, Enquirer, May 5, 1820, 3
Lang, George, Williamsburg, Enquirer, Jan. 1, 1824, 3
Lang, Mrs. Mary, Williamsburg, Enquirer, Sept. 14, 1821, 3
Lang, Wm., Manchester, Whig, Sept. 2, 1834, 3
Langhorn, Mrs. Elizabeth, Warwick, Enquirer, Aug. 18, 1818, 3
Langhorne, Mrs. Frances, Richmond, Whig, April 27, 1832, 1
Lanier, William, Petersburg, Enquirer, Oct. 1, 1813, 3
Laprade, Mrs. Susannah, Goochland, Enquirer, April 20, 1816, 3
Larne, Cadet of Norfolk, Enquirer, Dec. 18, 1813, 2
Laval, Col. Jacinth, Harper's Ferry, Enquirer, Sept. 13, 1822, 3
Law, Mrs., Franklin, Whig, Feb. 10, 1835, 3
Lawrence, William, Louisa, Enquirer, Nov. 21, 1806, 3
Lawson, Mrs. Mary, Prince William, Whig, May 9, 1837, 2
Laycock, Mrs. Phoebe, Westmoreland, Enquirer, Jan. 23, 25, 1823, 3
Layne, Charles, Sr., Campbell, Enquirer, June 8, 1821, 3
Lazerus, Joseph, Richmond, Enquirer, Nov. 25, 1817, 3
Leake, Mrs. Frances, Goochland, Enquirer, April 27, 1814, 4
Leake, Josiah, Jr., Hot Springs, Whig, Aug. 21, 1832, 1
Leake, Sarah H., Goochland, Enquirer, Sept. 21, 1819, 3
Lee, Mrs. Ann, Richmond, Whig, Jan. 28, 1832, 3
Lee, Col. Arthur, Norfolk, Enquirer, Jan. 22, 1828, 3
Lee, Baldwin M., Westmoreland, Enquirer, Feb. 26, 1822, 3
Lee, Daniel, Winchester, Whig, May 3, 1833, 1
Lee, Mrs. Elizabeth, Pittsylvania, Whig, Aug. 11, 1837, 2
Lee, John, Richmond, Enquirer, Sept. 26, 1823, 3
Lee, Lieut. John H., Norfolk, Whig, July 9, 1832, 1
Lee, Mrs. Mary L., Orange, Whig, April 8, 1836, 3
Lee, Richard, Northumberland, Enquirer, March 23, 1824, 3
Lee, Richard Henry, Richmond, Enquirer, Oct. 21, 1815, 3
Lee, Mrs. Sally, ————————, Whig, May 12, 1837, 2; May 19, 1837, 3
Lee, Mrs. Sarah, Northampton, Whig, July 21, 1827, 3
Lee, Sarah Ann, Richmond, Whig, Dec. 25, 1832, 3
Lee, Thomas Ludwell, Leesburg, Whig, Sept. 21, 1832, 1
Lee, Virginia Payne, Richmond, Whig, March 6, 1838, 2
Lee, William, near Charlestown, Whig, May 29, 1838, 2
Lee, William Fitzhugh, Richmond, Whig, May 23, 1837, 3
Lee, William Hancock, Manchester, Whig, May 1, 1835, 3
Lee, Wm. W., Warwick, Enquirer, April 16, 1814, 3

Leftwich, Capt. James, Lynchburg, Enquirer, Aug. 9, 1825; 3; Whig, Aug. 16, 1825, 3
Leftwich, Mrs. Sarah, Campbell, Whig, Oct. 5, 1829, 2
Leftwich, Mrs. Sarah P., Bedford, Whig, Nov. 3, 1837, 1
Leftwich, Dr. William, Pittsylvania, Enquirer, Oct. 13, 1818, 3
Legare, Mrs. Ann, —————, Whig, May 10, 1825, 3
Legge, Thos., Fredericksburg, Enquirer, Nov. 22, 1814, 3
Legrand, Lucy, Charlotte, Enquirer, Aug. 27, 1822, 3
LeGrand, Nash, Charlotte, Whig, Feb. 20, 1838, 1
Leneve, Edward, Richmond, Whig, Feb. 19, 1833, 3
Leneve, Samuel B., Richmond, Whig, Feb. 19, 1833, 3
Lenow, Wm., Southampton, Enquirer, Oct. 14, 1828, 3
Lester, Mrs. Jane, Richmond, Whig, Dec. 16, 1830, 3
Lester, Capt. John, Rocketts, Enquirer, Dec. 22, 1804, 3
Lester, Sarah, Richmond, Enquirer, May 18, 1816, 4
Levas, Ellen, Richmond, Whig, Oct. 19, 1832, 2
Levas, John, Richmond, Whig, Oct. 19, 1832, 2
Levas, Lucy, Richmond, Whig, Oct. 19, 1832, 2
Lewis, Mrs. Agnes, Charles City, Enquirer, Aug. 20, 1822, 3
Lewis, Dr. Alfred and Mrs. Elizabeth Travers, Spottsylvania, Enquirer, Aug. 28, 1827, 3
Lewis, Col. Andrew, Mason, Whig, June 11, 1833, 3
Lewis, Dr. Andrew, Botetourt, Enquirer, Oct. 11, 1822, 3
Lewis, Ann Marks, Albemarle, Whig, Oct. 29, 1833, 3
Lewis, Ann Overton, Spottsylvania, Enquirer, March 23, 1821, 3
Lewis, Burrell, New Kent, Enquirer, Aug. 13, 1824, 3
Lewis, Edward, —————, Enquirer, Oct. 5, 1827, 3
Lewis, Fielding, Charles City, Whig, June 24, 1834, 3
Lewis, Maj. George, Fredericksburg, Enquirer, Nov. 27, 1821, 3
Lewis, Howell, Mason, Enquirer, Jan. 13, 18, 1823, 3
Lewis, Mrs. Jane, Goochland, Enquirer, Feb. 21, 1818, 3
Lewis, Jane Elizabeth, Albemarle, Enquirer, July 12, 1811, 3
Lewis, Capt. John, Sweet Springs, Enquirer, June 24, 1823, 3
Lewis, John W., Mecklenburg, Whig, April 10, 1835, 1
Lewis, Joseph I., Culpeper, Enquirer, Dec. 23, 1824, 3
Lewis, Joseph J., Culpeper, Whig, Dec. 10, 1824, 3
Lewis, Matilda B., Albemarle, Enquirer, Nov. 2, 1819, 3
Lewis, Meriwether, —————, Enquirer, Nov. 17, 1809, 2 and 3
Lewis, Robert, Fredericksburg, Whig, Jan. 22, 1829, 3
Lewis, Capt. Thomas, Buckingham, Enquirer, Oct. 11, 1825, 3; Sept. 27, 1825, 3
Lewis, Dr. Thomas M., Westmoreland, Whig, Aug. 23, 1833, 1
Lewis, William, Buckingham, Whig, Sept. 15, 1837, 1
Lewry, Mrs. Anne Rebecca, Powhatan, Enquirer, Aug. 28, 1827, 3
Leyburn, Mrs. Ann Eliza, Lexington, Whig, Nov. 11, 1836, 1
Libby, Haskins, Richmond, Whig, July 6, 1838, 1
Libby, Seth, Richmond, Whig, Oct. 9, 1832, 1
Liggany, Capt., Westmoreland, Enquirer, July 20, 1813, 3
Lightfoot, Hon. Henry Benskin, —————, Enquirer, Nov. 19, 1805, 3

Lightfoot, Thomas Walker, Culpeper, Whig, March 12, 1831, 1
Lightfoot, Maj. William, —————, Enquirer, March 10, 1809, 3
Lightfoot, William, Sandy Point, Enquirer, July 25, 1809, 3
Ligon, John T., Prince Edward, Enquirer, May 14, 1822, 3
Linch, John, Lynchburg, Enquirer, Nov. 17, 1820, 3
Lindsay, Mrs. Mary Ann, Norfolk, Enquirer, Aug. 11, 1826, 3
Lindsay, Mrs. Mattie, Norfolk, Enquirer, Aug. 12, 1823, 3
Lindsay, William, Albemarle, Enquirer, Sept. 19, 1820, 3
Linn, James S., —————, Whig, Sept. 27, 1836, 3
Linscott, Edward, Portsmouth, Enquirer, June 8, 1827, 3
Lipscomb, Mrs. Harriet, —————, Enquirer, March 4, 1817, 3
Lipscomb, James Herbert, King William, Whig, April 3, 1838, 4
Lipscomb, Mrs. Letitia, Louisa, Enquirer, Dec. 16, 1826, 3
Lipscomb, Mrs. Lucy, King William, Enquirer, Aug. 20, 1811, 3
Littlepage, Isaac Burnley, King William, Enquirer, Jan. 13, 1814, 3
Lobb, Charles, Moorefield, Whig, March 24, 1837, 2
Lockheart, William, Richmond, Whig, Aug. 24, 1832, 1
Logan, Euselius, Augusta, Enquirer, Sept. 26, 1828, 3
Logwood, William, Chesterfield, Enquirer, Oct. 22, 1819, 3
Lomax, Sarah Maria, —————, Enquirer, Nov. 30, 1827, 3
Long, Maj. Gabriel, Culpeper, Enquirer, Feb. 20, 1827, 3
Lord, John, King William, Enquirer, Nov. 12, 1814, 3
Lord, Robinson, Henrico, Enquirer, July 23, 1819, 3
Love, Allen, Halifax, Enquirer, Feb. 22, 1817, 3
Lovelace, Mrs. Tabitha, Halifax, Whig, Oct. 8, 1833, 2
Lovelace, William O., Halifax, Enquirer, Aug. 15, 1826, 3
Low, Rev. Samuel, Norfolk, Enquirer, April 10, 1821, 3
Low, Rev. Samuel, Northumberland, Enquirer, July 16, 1814, 3
Lowe, Enoch M., Norfolk, Enquirer, March 4, 1823, 3
Lowkersley, Col. Reuben, Caroline, Enquirer, Sept. 30, 1823, 3
Lownes, James, [formerly of Virginia], Whig, Dec. 16, 1831, 1
Loyal, George M., Richmond, Whig, Sept. 27, 1830, 2
Lucas, —————, Norfolk, Enquirer, Aug. 28, 1821, 3
Lucas, Col. Edmund, Petersburg, Enquirer, Dec. 15, 1812, 3
Lucas, Virginia, Richmond, Whig, Jan. 5, 1838, 1
Luck, Samuel, Caroline, Whig, Jan. 23, 1838, 2
Lumpkin, C., —————, Enquirer, Oct. 25, 1822, 3
Lumpkin, Robert, Hanover, Enquirer, Oct. 19, 1824, 3
Lumsden, Wm., Richmond, Whig, June 8, 1830, 3
Lundy, Ethelred H., Greensville, Whig, Sept. 20, 1825, 3
Lyell, Mrs. Judith F., Richmond, Whig, July 18, 1837, 2
Lyle, John, Chesterfield, Enquirer, Sept. 7, 1827, 3
Lynch, James, Richmond, Whig, Aug. 19, 1825, 3
Lynch, John O., Richmond, Enquirer, Aug. 28, 1812, 3
Lyne, Col. William, King and Queen, Enquirer, Sept. 27, 1808, 3
Lyons, Mrs. Ann, Hanover, Enquirer, July 8, 1828, 3
Lyons, Hon. Peter, —————, Enquirer, Aug. 4, 1809, 3
Lyons, Robert S., Richmond, Whig, Aug. 9, 1836, 2

Mc.

McArthur, Mrs. Nancy, Fruit Hill, Whig, Nov. 8, 1836, 2
M'Carty, Robert W., Essex, Whig, April 11, 1826, 3
Macaulay, Francis, York Town, Enquirer, Oct. 22, 1811, 3
McCaw, John J., Richmond, Whig, April 25, 1831, 3
McCaw, Dr. Wm. Reid, Richmond, Whig, Sept. 29, 1837, 1
McBride, Mrs. Harriet, —————, Enquirer, Oct. 18, 1825, 3
McBride, John, Richmond, Whig, April 6, 1832, 1
McCabe, Mrs. Emily Agnes, Richmond, Whig, July 25, 1837, 2
McCabe, Mrs. Mary, Richmond, Whig, Jan. 20, 1831, 3
McCall, Archibald, Tappahannock, Enquirer, Nov. 1, 1814, 3
McCandish, Burwell Bassett, Henrico, Whig, Aug. 13, 1833, 2
McCandlish, Mrs. Elizabeth, Williamsburg, Whig, June 2, 1830, 3
McCarty, Col. Edward, Hampshire, Enquirer, Sept. 24, 1824, 3
McCarty, George, Fairfax, Enquirer, Sept. 27, 1808, 3
M'Chesney, William, Fluvanna, Enquirer, Oct. 19, 1816, 3
McCleland, John Milton, Nelson, Whig, June 16, 1835, 3
M'Clurg, Mrs., Richmond, Enquirer, July 1, 1815, 3
McClurg, Dr. James, Richmond, Enquirer, July 11, 1823, 3
McConnico, Col. Andrew J., Norfolk, Whig, Nov. 29, 1830, 3
McCormick, John, Buckingham, Enquirer, Nov. 3, 8, 1822, 3
McCormick, Mrs. Mary E., Buckingham, Enquirer, April 12, 1822, 3
McCormick, Mrs. Susan, Buckingham, Enquirer, Aug. 16, 1822, 3
McCoull, James, Fredericksburg, Whig, Jan. 9, 1838, 4
McCoull, Mrs. Julia, Richmond, Whig, March 8, 1836, 3
M'Coull, Neill, Marion Hill, Whig, June 6, 1826, 3
McCraw, Mrs. Emily, Richmond, Enquirer, March 29, 1808, 3
McCraw, Mrs. Emily Fowler, Richmond, Enquirer, Dec. 23, 1817, 3
McCraw, Frances, Buckingham, Whig, Oct. 17, 1834, 1
McCraw, Samuel, Richmond, Enquirer, June 24, 1823, 3
McCredie, John, Richmond, Enquirer, Feb. 6, 10, 1807, 3
McCredie, Mrs. Nancy, Richmond, Enquirer, June 28, 1822, 3
McCue, John, Fredericksburg, Enquirer, Oct. 2, 1818, 3
McCulloch, Mrs. Mary W., Amherst, Enquirer, Feb. 18, 1819, 3
McCurdy, Mrs. Teriss, Richmond, Whig, March 8, 1838, 2
M'Donough, E. H., Mason, Enquirer, Sept. 20, 1825, 3
McDougle, James, Enquirer, Oct. 4, 1822, 3
McDowell, Louis Marshall, Rockbridge, Whig, Nov. 13, 1832, 3
McEnery, William, Richmond, Whig, March 22, 1825, 3
MacFarlan, Mrs. Phoebe A., Richmond, Whig, Aug. 22, 1826, 3
Macfarland, Mrs. Ann T., Richmond, Whig, Jan. 4, 1833, 3
MacFarland, James, Lunenburg, Whig, April 25, 1837, 3
MacFarland, Mrs. Mary, Dinwiddie, Enquirer, July 7, 1826, 3
M'Farlane, Wm., Fredericksburg, Whig, Nov. 22, 1825, 3
McGee, Col. Robert, Williamsburg, Enquirer, April 20, 1821, 2
M'Gillespie, John, Richmond, Enquirer, Jan. 30, 1821, 3
Macgruder, Mrs. Sarah B., Fluvanna, Whig, June 3, 1836, 4
McHenry, John, Richmond, Enquirer, Nov. 1, 1814, 3

M'Kein, Jane Ann, Petersburg, Enquirer, Aug. 14, 1821, 3
M'Kenney, Mrs. Martha P., Charlotte, Enquirer, July 9, 1819, 3
McKensie, William, Richmond, Whig, June 10, 1829, 3
McKenzie, Wm., New Kent, Enquirer, Oct. 6, 1826, 3
M'kim, Mrs. Elizabeth, Richmond, Whig, Jan. 11, 1830, 3
McKoon, Capt. John, Virginia, Enquirer, July 25, 1817, 3
M'laughlin, Dennis, Richmond, Enquirer, Aug. 28, 1818, 3
McLaurin, Capt. Joseph, Norfolk, Enquirer, Sept. 24, 1814, 3
M'Laurine, Mrs. Harriet, Powhatan, Enquirer, Feb. 18, 1826, 3
McLaurine, Mrs. Susannah, Cumberland, Enquirer, June 5, 1821, 3
McLein, Mrs. Mary, Goochland, Enquirer, Feb. 19, 1824, 3
M'Lelland, Capt., ————, Whig, July 19, 1830, 3
Maclin, Col. John D., Greensville, Whig, March 8, 1836, 3
M'Morrough, Dr. John M., [formerly of Virginia], Whig, Oct. 10, 1834, 4
Macmurdo, Robert W., Richmond, Whig, July 27, 1836, 4
Macmurdo, Thomas, Richmond, Whig, March 25, 1825, 3
McMurdo, Thomas Bolling, Richmond, Whig, July 14, 1837, 4
Macnair, Ebenezer, Richmond, Enquirer, Aug. 10, 1821, 3
McNaught, James, Richmond, Enquirer, March 2, 1826, 3
McNemara, Joseph M., Richmond, Whig, Aug. 25, 1831, 2
McNemara, Mrs. Lucy Ann P., Richmond, Whig, May 9, 1834, 1
Macomb, Aleaxander, Georgetown, Whig, Jan. 25, 1831, 3
Macon, Col. Edgar, ————, Whig, Dec. 19, 1829, 3
Macon, Mrs. Hannah, New Kent, Enquirer, Sept. 28, 1813, 3
Macon, Mrs. Lucy Ann, Powhatan, Whig, May 1, 1835, 1
Macon, Sarah Elizabeth, Orange, Whig, July 25, 1831, 4
Macon, Col. William, Hanover, Enquirer, Nov. 30, 1813, 3
M'Rae, Allan, Chesterfield, Enquirer, Dec. 13, 1825, 3
McRae, Rev. Christopher, ————, Enquirer, Dec. 31, 1808, 3
Macrae, John, Fauquier, Whig, Jan. 18, 1830, 3
McRae, Mrs. Judith J., Manchester, Whig, Jan. 24, 1832, 1
McRae, Tabitha R., Chesterfield, Whig, May 11, 1838, 2
McRobert, Col. Archibald, Prince Edward, Enquirer, Oct. 16, 1824, 3

M.

Maddox, John, Richmond, Whig, July 25, 1834, 2
Madison, Alfred, ————, Enquirer, Feb. 12, 1811, 3
Madison, Mrs. Eleanor, Montpelier, Whig, Feb. 19, 1829, 3
Madison, Bishop James, ————, Enquirer, March 13, 1812, 4
Madison, Capt. James, Caroline, Whig, Oct. 17, 1829, 3
Madison, James Edwin, Madison, Enquirer, Oct. 19, 1821, 3
Madison, John, Orange, Enquirer, April 7, 1809, 3
Madison, Lucy Frances, Madison, Enquirer, Jan. 20, 1814, 3
Madison, Pamela, Louisa, Enquirer, Dec. 29, 1810, 3
Madison, Robert L., Culpeper, Enquirer, Feb. 23, 1828, 3; Whig, March 1, 1828, 3
Madison, Mrs. Sarah, Williamsburg, Enquirer, Aug. 26, 1815, 3
Magee, Mrs. Ann, Richmond, Whig, April 28, 1837, 2

Magiel, Archibald, Frederick, Enquirer, Feb. 15, 1821, 3
Magill, Catherine, Williamsburg, Enquirer, Aug. 21, 1821, 3
Magruder, Sally Watson, Fluvanna, Whig, Dec. 15, 1835, 3
Magruder, Sarah Eliza Timberlake, Botetourt, Whig, Aug. 7, 1838, 2
Magruder, Wm. B., Caroline, Whig, Sept. 24, 1833, 1
Malloch, Joseph, Albemarle, Enquirer, July 3, 1818, 3
Mann, Benjamin, Richmond, Whig, March 31, 1835, 3
Mann, Mrs. Elizabeth Ann, Richmond, Whig, April 28, 1835, 2
Mann, James H., Richmond, Whig, Jan. 27, 1831, 2
Mare, Dr. William B., Nelson, Enquirer, Sept. 1, 1818, 3
Marks, Henry, Richmond, Enquirer, March 17, 1809, 3
Marks, Solomon, Jr., Norfolk, Whig, Aug. 25, 1827, 3
Marquis, James, Richmond, Whig, Sept. 1, 1831, 2
Marrow, John, Warwick, Whig, Dec. 16, 1825, 3
Marsey, Chás., Sr., King George, Enquirer, July 6, 1821, 3
Marshal, William, Hanover, Whig, Sept. 7, 1824, 3
Marshall, Almerine, Wythe, Enquirer, Jan. 4, 1812, 3
Marshall, Mrs. Catharine, Winchester, Enquirer, Sept. 26, 1826, 3
Marshall, James Edgar, Fredericksburg, Enquirer, Nov. 8, 1825, 3; Whig, Nov. 8, 1825, 3
Marshall, Chief Justice John, Richmond, Whig, July 10, 1835, 2
Marshall, Louis, Rockbridge, Whig, Nov. 13, 1832, 3
Marshall, Mary, Richmond, Enquirer, Jan. 7, 1812, 3
Marshall, Mrs. Mary W., Richmond, Whig, Dec. 30, 1831, 1
Marshall, Thomas, Mecklenburg, Whig, Feb. 13, 1838, 2
Marshall, Thomas, Pittsylvania, Whig, April 20, 1838, 4
Marshall, Thomas, Winchester, Enquirer, Sept. 28, 1826, 3
Marshall, William, Richmond, Enquirer, May 29, 1816, 3
Martin, Mrs. Ann F., Chesterfield, Enquirer, June 17, 1828, 3
Martin, Mrs. James [Susan], Henry, Whig, April 18, 1837, 4
Martin, Gen. Joseph, Henry, Enquirer, Jan. 7, 10, 1809, 3
Martin, Julius, New Kent, Enquirer, Aug. 30, 1822, 3; Sept. 3, 1822, 3
Martin, Mary, Richmond, Whig, Dec. 20, 1836, 3
Martin, Maj. Thomas, ————, Enquirer, Feb. 11, 1819, 4
Martin, William, Chesterfield, Enquirer, Jan. 31, 1824, 3
Martyr, Richard Henry, Richmond, Whig, May 10, 1825, 3
Marx, Mrs. Fanny, Richmond, Enquirer, July 13, 1819, 3
Marx, Richa, Richmond, Whig, March 24, 1838, 2
Marx, Wilhelmina, Richmond, Whig, July 6, 1836, 3
Mason, Alexander Kosciusko, King George, Enquirer, July 6, 1821, 4
Mason, Mrs. Jane T., Richmond, Whig, Aug. 16, 1825, 3
Mason, John, King and Queen, Enquirer, July 25, 1828, 3; Aug. 22, 1828, 3
Mason, John MaCarty, Fairfax, Whig, July 14, 1837, 4
Mason, Robert H., Greenville, Whig, Sept. 15, 1827, 3
Mason, Virginia, Hollins Hall, Whig, Jan. 30, 1838, 1
Massey, Chas., Sr., King George, Enquirer, July 6, 1821, 3
Massey, Robert B., King George, Enquirer, Oct. 19, 1816, 3
Massie, Eliza Logan, Richmond, Whig, Jan. 12, 1838, 2
Massie, Mrs. Lucy, Nelson, Enquirer, Sept. 10, 1822, 3

Massie, Martha, Richmond, Enquirer, Feb. 12, 1824, 3
Massie, Mrs. Martha, Lynchburg, Whig, July 9, 1832, 3
Massie, Mrs. Susan Preston, Albemarle, Enquirer, Dec. 28, 1825, 3; Jan.
    5, 1826, 3
Mathews, James, Hanover, Enquirer, Oct. 4, 1819, 3
Matthews, Mary, Hanover, Enquirer, Sept. 25, 1827, 3
Matthews, Wm., Powhatan, Whig, April 10, 1830, 3
Matthews, Wm. B., Richmond, Whig, Nov. 6, 1830, 3
Mattox, Mrs. Edwin A. [Mildred], Richmond, Whig, Feb. 3, 1837, 1
Maule, Mrs. Margaret, Richmond, Whig, Jan. 28, 1835, 3
Maury, Fontaine, Fredericksburg, Enquirer, Feb. 3, 1824, 3
Maxey, Rev. Elisha, Powhatan, Enquirer, Oct. 19, 1824, 3
Maxey, Mrs. Sarah, Powhatan, Whig, May 17, 1836, 2 .
Mayo, Agnes P., Richmond, Whig, March 7, 1831, 3
Mayo, Alexander Fulton, Richmond, Whig, Oct. 29, 1830, 3
Mayo, Charlotte, Richmond, Whig, July 29, 1834, 1
Mayo, Mrs. Dorathea, Richmond, Whig, March 5, 1831, 2
Mayo, Elizabeth P., Richmond, Whig, Dec. 16, 1836, 2
Mayo, Mrs. Jane, Fauquier, Whig, March 24, 1837, 1
Mayo, Joseph H., Richmond, Whig, Nov. 17, 1828, 3
Mayo, Louisa, Richmond, Enquirer, Jan. 2, 1812, 3
Mayo, Mrs. Mary E., Washington, Enquirer, Jan. 21, 1823, 3
Mays, Susannah, Mathews, Enquirer, Dec. 17, 1822, 3
Mead, Amzi Stockton, Richmond, Whig, Aug. 3, 1832, 3
Meade, Richard Kidder, Frederick, Whig, March 12, 1833, 3
Meade, Sarah Rutherford, Amelia, Whig, March 8, 1833, 3
Meade, Mrs. Thomasia, Hanover, Whig, Aug. 5, 1836, 1
Meanley, Archilus, Richmond, Whig, Oct. 5, 1832, 1
Meaux, Mrs. Lucy A., King William, Enquirer, Oct. 5, 1824, 3
Meaux, Mrs. Mary O., Caroline, Whig, Sept. 30, 1825, 3; Enquirer, Oct.
    4, 1825, 3
Megginson, Mrs. Sarah, Nelson, Whig, Dec. 29, 1837, 2
Meigs, Return J., —————, Enquirer, April 12, 1825, 3
Meltauer, Mrs. Mary, Prince Edward, Enquirer, Dec. 11, 1823, 3
Mennis, Callohill, Bedford, Whig, Dec. 28, 1829, 3
Mercer, Gen., —————, Enquirer, Feb. 18, 1826, 3
Mercer, Col. John, —————, Enquirer, Oct. 21, 1817, 3
Mercer, Col. John F., —————, Enquirer, Sept. 14, 1821, 3
Meredith, Mrs. Ann E., Richmond, Whig, Nov. 27, 1835, 2
Meredith, Mrs. Ann L., Hanover, Enquirer, Sept. 11, 1816, 3
Meriam, John, Richmond, Whig, Nov. 21, 1827, 3
Meriam, John Adams, Richmond, Whig, Oct. 1, 1833, 2
Meredith, Col. Samuel, Amherst, Enquirer, Jan. 19, 1809, 2
Meredith, Samuel, New Kent, Whig, Feb. 6, 1838, 2
Meredith, Wm., Richmond, Enquirer, March 6, 1812, 3
Meridith, Elizabeth K., Hanover, Enquirer, June 20, 1817, 3
Merton, Mrs. Nancy J., Richmond, Whig, Oct. 8, 1830, 3
Merton, Wm., Richmond, Whig, Dec. 5, 1834, 3
Mewburn, Mrs. Sarah R., Goochland, Whig, Aug. 14, 1829, 3

Michaels, Mrs. Mary B., Manchester, Enquirer, Sept. 26, 1823, 3
Michaux, Ann, Pittsylvania, Whig, July 28, 1831, 1
Michie, Robert, Hanover, Enquirer, May 6, 1828, 3
Micou, Paul, Jr., Essex, Enquirer, July 17, 1821, 3
Middleton, Elizabeth A., Rocketts, Whig, Sept. 28, 1829, 3
Mieure, Mrs. Mary R., Richmond, Whig, April 20, 1832, 1
Migginson, Mrs. Almira, Nelson, Whig, April 22, 1830, 3
Milcap, James, Manchester, Enquirer, July 24, 1827, 3
Miles, S., Petersburg, Enquirer, Oct. 1, 1813, 3
Mill, Rev. John, King William, Enquirer, Oct. 21, 1825, 3
Millar, Nelson, Norfolk, Enquirer, Sept. 20, 1825, 3
Miller, Mrs. Catherine T., Powhatan, Enquirer, June 30, 1826, 3
Miller, Col. Heath, Goochland, Enquirer, Feb. 14, 1818, 3
Miller, Joseph K., Richmond, Enquirer, Oct. 27, 1826, 3
Miller, Col. Peter, Richmond, Whig, March 5, 1832, 3
Miller, Thomas, Goochland, Enquirer, May 7, 1819, 3
Miller, William Heath, Goochland, Enquirer, June 10, 1815, 3
Mills, Ann Eliza, Louisa, Whig, March 12, 1836, 3
Mills, Charles H., Louisa, Whig, March 12, 1836, 3
Mills, Mrs. Isabella A., Louisa, Whig, Sept. 20, 1836, 2
Milly, Wm. Surry, Whig, March 1, 1828, 3
Mims, Martin, Goochland, Enquirer, Sept. 28, 1819, 3
Mims, Mrs. Susan R., Manchester, Whig, May 16, 1834, 2
Miner, Daniel, Buckingham, Whig, Aug. 14, 1838, 4
Miner, Peter, Albemarle, Enquirer, April 24, 1827, 3
Minge, John, Charles City, Whig, June 5, 1827, 3
Mink, George, Lehigh, Whig, May 13, 1830, 3
Minor, Dabney, Orange, Enquirer, March 15, 1822, 3
Minor, Mrs. Jane, Tappahannock, Enquirer, March 19, 1824, 3
Minor, Gen. John, Fredericksburg, Enquirer, June 12, 1816, 3
Minor, Mrs. Nancy D., Caroline, Enquirer, Oct. 5, 9, 1821, 3
Minor, Virginia, Richmond, Whig, Nov. 4, 1836, 3
Minton, Col. John, Nansemond, Whig, April 17, 1830, 3
Minton, Mrs. Sarah B., Henrico, Enquirer, Jan. 15, 1828, 3
Mishads, Mrs. Mary B., Manchester, Enquirer, Sept. 26, 1823, 3
Mitchell, Capt., Richmond, Enquirer, July 25, 1820, 3
Mitchell, Mrs. Ann, Henrico, Enquirer, March 23, 1827, 3
Mitchell, Dr. Chas. L., [formerly of Lynchburg], Enquirer, Sept. 9, 1823, 3
Mitchell, Hestilene Matilda, Richmond, Whig, Aug. 21, 1838, 2
Mitchell, James, King and Queen, Enquirer, Oct. 12, 1821, 3
Mitchell, Reuben, Richmond, Whig, Nov. 1, 1828, 3
Mitchell, Capt. Robert, Richmond, Enquirer, Jan. 3, 1811, 3
Mitchell, William, Louisa, Enquirer, Dec. 5, 1822, 3
Mitchill, Dr. Samuel L., Richmond, Whig, Sept. 12, 1831, 4
Molley, David, Cumberland, Enquirer, May 12, 1826, 3
Moncure, Mrs. Esther J., Stafford, Whig, June 14, 1833, 3
Moncure, Frances Ann, Stafford, Whig, March 15, 1833, 1
Moncure, John Stafford, Enquirer, Aug. 20, 1822, 3
Moncure, John James, Richmond, Whig, Aug. 19, 1829, 3

Moncure, William, Richmond, Whig, Nov. 14, 1831, 3
Moncure, Wm. R., Stafford, Enquirer, April 18, 1828, 3; Whig, April 23, 1828, 3
Monroe, Andrew, Charlottesville, Enquirer, Dec. 16, 1826, 3
Monroe, Andrew Milton, —————, Enquirer, Dec. 16, 1826, 3
Monroe, Benj. James, Westmoreland, Whig, Aug. 25, 1829, 3
Monroe, Joseph Jones, —————, Enquirer, Aug. 27, 1824, 3
Montague, Mrs. Catherine, Middlesex, Enquirer, March 2, 1824, 3
Montague, Elizabeth Rebecca, —————, Enquirer, March 16, 1824, 3
Montague, George W., Powhatan, Enquirer, Jan. 5, 1821, 3
Montague, John, [formerly of Virginia], Whig, Oct. 6, 1831, 4
Montague, Capt. Mikelborough, Powhatan, Enquirer, Jan. 3, 1828, 3
Montague, Peter, Powhatan, Enquirer, Feb. 4, 1823, 3
Montague, William, Henrico, Enquirer, Aug. 3, 1827, 3
Montell, John, Richmond, Whig, April 19, 1834, 1
Montgomery, Dr. Wm. H., Lexington, Enquirer, April 14, 1826, 3
Moody, Mrs. Ann T., Williamsburg, Whig, Aug. 29, 1837, 1
Moody, Blanks, Surry, Enquirer, Dec. 11, 1823, 3
Moody, Mrs. Elizabeth Pope, Richmond, Enquirer, Sept. 26, 1820, 3
Moody, Capt. John, Richmond, Whig, Sept. 26, 1826, 3; Enquirer, Oct. 3, 1826, 3
Moody, Mary E., Chesterfield, Whig, Nov. 14, 1837, 1
Moody, Robert, Richmond, Enquirer, Sept. 8, 1812, 3
Moody, William, Powhatan, Enquirer, Oct. 21, 1823, 3
Moon, Littleberry, Albemarle, Whig, Jan. 23, 1827, 3; Enquirer, Jan. 27, 1827, 3
Moore, A. L., King William, Enquirer, March 28, 1828, 3
Moore, Gen. Andrew, Rockbridge, Enquirer, June 5, 1821, 3
Moore, Mrs. Channing, Richmond, Enquirer, Aug. 10, 1824, 3
Moore, Curtis R., Richmond, Enquirer, March 9, 1814, 3
Moore, Frances Anne, King and Queen, Enquirer, June 24, 1828, 3
Moore, Hardin P., Bedford, Enquirer, Dec. 25, 1824, 3
Moore, Peter, Richmond, Enquirer, May 24, 1822, 3
Moore, Thomas, —————, Enquirer, Oct. 8, 29, 1822, 3
Morgan, Daniel, Shepherdstown, Whig, Jan. 13, 1837, 1
Morgan, Mrs. Diana, —————, Enquirer, March 5, 1822, 3
Morris, George, Amherst, Enquirer, Sept. 19, 1826, 3
Morris, Hardenia, Hanover, Enquirer, Nov. 22, 1811, 3
Morris, Mrs. Mary W., Hanover, Whig, Nov. 13, 1835, 4
Morris, Peter, Amherst, Enquirer, Sept. 19, 1826, 3
Morris, Rachel, Amherst, Enquirer, Sept. 19, 1826, 3
Morris, Mrs. Sarah, Nottoway, Enquirer, Oct. 6, 1826, 3
Morris, Wm., Louisa, Whig, Feb. 7, 1831, 3
Morris, William, Hanover, Enquirer, May 2, 1820, 3
Morris, William O., Louisa, Enquirer, Sept. 28, 1819, 3
Morrison, Mrs. Ann, Louisa, Whig, Aug. 2, 1836, 1
Morrison, Brokenbrough S., Powhatan, Whig, April 8, 1836, 3
Morrison, Mrs. Martha C., Pittsylvania, Whig, Jan. 27, 1837, 4
Morrison, Mrs. Mildred, Albemarle, Whig, Sept. 24, 1833, 3

Morriss, Edward, New Kent, Enquirer, Aug. 2, 1822, 3
Morriss, George, Rachel and Peter, Amherst, Enquirer, Sept. 19, 1826, 3
Morriss, Henry, Gloucester, Enquirer, Oct. 9, 1810, 3
Morriss, Mrs. Matilda, Gloucester, Enquirer, Nov. 12, 1819, 3
Morriss, Samuel C., Gloucester, Enquirer, Nov. 12, 1819, 3
Morse, Ebenezer, —————, Enquirer, Aug. 27, 1824, 3
Morton, Mrs. Ann, Richmond, Whig, April 3, 1829, 3
Morton, Col. William, Charlotte, Enquirer, Dec. 21, 1820, 3
Mosby, Dr. Edward, Louisa, Enquirer, March 5, 1822, 3
Mosby, John Wade, Powhatan, Whig, July 30, 1833, 3
Mosby, Gen. Littleberry, Powhatan, Enquirer, Oct. 26, 1821, 3
Mosby, Mary, Henrico, Whig, Jan. 18, 1825, 3
Mosby, Mrs. Mary H., Richmond, Whig, Nov. 10, 1831, 4
Mosby, Samuel, Hanover, Whig, Feb. 7, 1829, 2
Mosby, Wade, Sr., Powhatan, Whig, June 13, 1834, 2
Mosby, Wm. O., Goochland, Whig, Nov. 1, 1830, 3
Moseley, Mrs. Ann, Charlotte, Enquirer, Aug. 13, 1826, 3
Moseley, Mary Caroline, Buckingham, Whig, March 28, 1837, 4
Moseley, Peter, Richmond, Enquirer, Jan. 14, 1813, 3
Moseley, Sarah, Manchester, Enquirer, Oct. 29, 1822, 3
Moseley, Mrs. Susanna, Buckingham, Whig, Sept. 2, 1834, 3
Moseley, William, Powhatan, Whig, May 25, 1838, 2
Moseley, Gen. William, Richmond, Enquirer, Oct. 7, 1808, 3
Mosely, Mrs. Ann, Charlotte, Enquirer, Aug. 18, 1826, 3
Mosely, Mrs. Mary, Richmond, Enquirer, Jan. 17, 1824, 3
Mosely, Richard, Hanover, Enquirer, Oct. 26, 1824, 3
Mosley, Mrs. Mary, Richmond, Enquirer, Jan. 17, 1824, 3
Moss, Benjamin W., Petersburg, Whig, May 1, 1832, 1
Moss, Maj. Hugh, Powhatan, Enquirer, July 3, 6, 1810, 3
Moss, Richard Henry, Richmond, Enquirer, Dec. 25, 1824, 3
Moss, Samuel, New Kent, Enquirer, July 3, 1827, 3
Motley, Mrs. Mary Ann, Caroline, Whig, April 10, 1835, 1
Motley, William, Petersburg, Enquirer, Sept. 9, 1815, 3
Mott, Thomas R., Monroe, Enquirer, Aug. 15, 1826, 3
Muhlenberg, Gen. Peter, —————, Enquirer, Oct. 14, 1807, 4
Muir, Mrs. Mary, Dinwiddie, Enquirer, Jan. 10, 1824, 3
Muire, Mrs. Ann, King and Queen, Enquirer, Sept. 26, 1826, 3
Mumford, Mrs. Angelica, Powhatan, Enquirer, May 23, 1828, 3
Mumford, Sally Ann, Powhatan, Whig, Nov. 23, 1824, 3
Mumford, William, Richmond, Whig, June 24, 1825, 3
Mundin, Mrs. Mary, Richmond, Whig, April 24, 1834, 1
Munford, Mrs. Elizabeth M., Richmond, Whig, Aug. 2, 1836, 2
Munford, Mrs. Lucy S., Richmond, Whig, June 19, 1835, 1
Munford, Mrs. Sarah, Buckingham, Whig, June 19, 1832, 4
Munford, William, Richmond, Enquirer, June 24, 1825, 3
Murchie, John, Chesterfield, Whig, March 23, 1831, 3
Murdaugh, Josiah, Nansemond, Enquirer, Feb. 14, 1826, 3
Murdauh, Dr. John, Nansemond, Whig, Jan. 18, 1830, 3
Murphy, Dolly, Buckingham, Whig, July 3, 1838, 4

Murray, Bolling, Powhatan, Enquirer, Aug. 17, 1821, 3
Murray, Mrs. Rebecca, Amelia, Enquirer, Oct. 10, 1826, 3
Mus, Daniel, Northumberland, Enquirer, Dec. 2, 1825, 3
Muschett, Dr. Alexander, Dumfries, Enquirer, Feb. 20, 1832, 3
Muse, Wm. T., [formerly of Westmoreland], Enquirer, Aug. 8, 1823, 3
Muse, Mrs. Jane, Tappahannock, Enquirer, Nov. 24, 1807, 3
Mutter, Mrs. John, Richmond, Enquirer, Oct. 22, 1814, 3
Myers, Mrs. Elizabeth, Norfolk, Enquirer, Nov. 4, 1823, 3
Myers, Mrs. Elizabeth, Richmond, Whig, Oct. 30, 1835, 2
Myers, Frederick, Richmond, Whig, June 22, 1832, 3
Myers, John, Norfolk, Whig, Dec. 4, 1830, 3
Myers, Capt. John A., Richmond, Whig, Oct. 3, 1827, 3
Myers, John S., Richmond, Whig, July 8, 1836, 1
Myers, Joseph M., Manchester, Enquirer, Sept. 12, 1817, 3
Myers, Mrs. Joyce, ————, Enquirer, July 30, 1824, 3
Myers, Moses, Richmond, Whig, July 14, 1835, 1
Myers, Mrs. Sally Hays, Richmond, Whig, Aug. 7, 1832, 1

N.

Napier, Capt. John, Fluvanna, Enquirer, Feb. 18, 1806, 3
Naylor, Mary, Romney, Whig, Jan. 16, 1838, 1
Neal, Mrs. Nelley L., Pittsylvania, Whig, Feb. 27, 1838, 1
Neale, Henry, Richmond, Whig, Feb. 23, 1836, 3
Neale, Wm., Richmond, Whig, April 3, 1829, 3
Neilson, Mrs. Edmonia Lee, Frederick, Whig, Dec. 23, 1834, 3
Neilson, Eliza, Richmond, Enquirer, Aug. 9, 1815, 3
Neilson, Isabella, Richmond, Whig, Feb. 11, 1825, 3
Neilson, Robert, [formerly of Richmond], Whig, July 16, 1833, 1
Neilson, Wm. H., [formerly of Norfolk], Whig, May 13, 1834, 2
Nelson, Charlotte S., Albemarle, Whig, Aug. 9, 1833, 3
Nelson, Mrs. Francis A. T., Richmond, Whig, Sept. 17, 1828, 3; Enquirer,
    Sept. 16, 1828, 3
Nelson, Maj. John, Mecklenburg, Enquirer, March 10, 1827, 3
Nelson, Mrs. Judith, Richmond, Enquirer, March 30, 1827, 3
Nelson, Judith Jane, Richmond, Whig, Feb. 15, 1833, 4
Nelson, Mrs. Lucy, Charles City, Whig, May 2, 1834, 2
Nelson, Mrs. Lucy, Hanover, Whig, Sept. 22, 1830, 3
Nelson, Mrs. Lucy, King William, Enquirer, April 20, 1810, 3
Nelson, Rev. Peter, Hanover, Whig, March 14, 1827, 3; Enquirer, March
    8, 1827, 3
Nelson, Robert, Malvern Hills, Enquirer, Aug. 11, 1818, 3
Nelson, Robert, Williamsburg, Enquirer, July 14, 1818, 3
Nelson, Mrs. Sarah, King William, Enquirer, Oct. 11, 1825, 3
Nelson, Thomas, Hanover, Enquirer, June 11, 1824, 3
Nelson, Hon. William, Williamsburg, Enquirer, March 16, 23, 1813, 3
New, George R., Richmond, Whig, Nov. 14, 1837, 1
Newman, Dr. Granville, Richmond, Whig, Aug. 16, 1825, 3
Newsum, Mary, Surry, Whig, May 6, 1825, 3

Newton, Mrs. Sally, Westmoreland, Enquirer, June 13, 1828, 3
Newton, Thomas F., Westmoreland, Enquirer, Feb. 20, 1827, 3
Niblet, Solomon, —————, Enquirer, Nov. 11, 1815, 3
Niblock, Dr. James, Brunswick, Enquirer, July 20, 1810, 3
Nice, Dr. Wm. G., Powhatan, Enquirer, Oct. 4, 1822, 3
Nicholas, Charles J., Richmond, Whig, Oct. 20, 1835, 4
Nicholas, Dr. George D., Middlesex, Enquirer, April 3, 1823, 3
Nicholas, George W., Williamsburg, Whig, Oct. 6, 1831, 4
Nicholas, George W., —————, Enquirer, Sept. 12, 1809, 3
Nicholas, Col. John, Dinwiddie, Enquirer, Feb. 26, 1818, 3
Nicholas, John Ambler, Richmond, Whig, Jan. 24, 1832, 1
Nicholas, Louisa H., Buckingham, Enquirer, Sept. 28, 1821, 3
Nicholas, Mrs. Mary, —————, Enquirer, May 2, 1820, 3
Nicholas, Nelson, —————, Enquirer, Aug. 11, 1826, 3
Nicholas, Nelson, New Canton, Enquirer, Oct. 5, 1821, 3
Nicholas, Sally, Surry, Enquirer, July 13, 1810, 3
Nicholas, Col. Wilson C., —————, Enquirer, Oct. 17, 1820, 3
Nicholas, Wilson Cary, —————, Whig, Aug. 27, 1828, 3; Enquirer,
    Sept. 5, 1828, 3
Nicolson, Dr. George D., Middlesex, Enquirer, April 3, 1823, 3
Nocolson [Nicolson], Thomas, Richmond, Enquirer, Nov. 18, 1808, 3
Niveson, William T., Norfolk, Enquirer, Oct. 26, 1821, 3
Nixon, Robert S., —————, Enquirer, Dec. 8, 1818, 3
Noble, James, Richmond, Whig, March 2, 1831, 3
Norris, Rev. Oliver, Alexandria, Whig, Aug. 26, 1825, 3
Norris, Mrs. Sarah Fairfax, Alexandria, Enquirer, Sept. 26, 1823, 3
North, Abraham R., Lynchburg, Whig, May 19, 1837, 1
Norvell, Wm., Lynchburg, Enquirer, Nov. 4, 1823, 3
Nott, Robert, Richmond, Whig, July 30, 1833, 3
Nunn, William B., King and Queen, Enquirer, Sept. 18, 1827, 3
Nunnally, Patrick Henry, Richmond, Whig, Feb. 23, 1833, 3
Nunnally, Spencer, Richmond, Whig, April 10, 1832, 3

O.

O'Connor, Eliza, Norfolk, Enquirer, June 18, 1811, 2
O'Connor, James, Norfolk, Enquirer, July 13, 1819, 3
O'Donnell, Francis B., [formerly of Lynchburg], Whig, Sept. 28, 1830, 3
Ogilvie, Mrs. James, Richmond, Enquirer, March 12, 1805, 3
Oldham, Edward, King George, Whig, March 17, 1835, 3
Oliver, Benjamin, Hanover, Enquirer, Dec. 24, 1818, 3
Oliver, Benjamin, Hanover, Enquirer, Sept. 19, 1820, 3
Oliver, John, Hanover, Enquirer, Feb. 4, 1815, 3
Oliver, Richard W., Nottoway, Whig, Sept. 26, 1837, 2
Olphin, Rebeca, Richmond, Whig, Nov. 1, 1824, 3
Opie, Mrs. Margaret, Jefferson, Whig, March 8, 1830, 3
Orgain, Anna A., Surry, Whig, Sept. 2, 1836, 4
Oswald, James A., Richmond, Whig, May 21, 1833, 2
Overton, Judge, Louisa, Whig, May 3, 1833, 1

Overton, Capt. James, Louisa, Enquirer, Feb. 17, 1816, 3
Overton, Col. John, ――――――, Enquirer, May 7, 1822, 3
Owen, Christopher, Urbanna, Enquirer, Dec. 7, 1820, 3
Owen, George W., Richmond, Whig, Sept. 1, 1837, 4
Owen, Mrs. Martha, Urbanna, Enquirer, Dec. 7, 1820, 3
Owen, Robertson, Halifax, Enquirer, Feb. 23, 1819, 3

P.

Pae, Thomas, Richmond, Whig, Aug. 7, 1838, 2,
Page, Carter, Cumberland, Enquirer, April 22, 1825, 3
Page, Carter B., Norfolk, Enquirer, Sept. 7, 10, 1824, 3
Page, Cary Selden, Jefferson, Whig, Oct. 6, 1837, 4
Page, Charles C., King William, Enquirer, Oct. 29, 1822, 3
Page, Ellen Cary, Cumberland, Whig, May 26, 1837, 1
Page, Jane Byrd, Fairfield, Enquirer, July 1, 1828, 3
Page, Hon. John, Gloucester, Enquirer, Oct. 14, 1808, 3
Page, Mrs. John M., Hanover, Whig, April 20, 1831, 4
Page, Mrs. Margaret, Williamsburg, Whig, Oct. 26, 1835, 2
Page, Mrs. Mildred, Richmond, Enquirer, Oct. 13, 1826, 3
Page, Octavius Augustus, ――――――, Enquirer, June 15, 1813, 3
Page, Wm. Byrd, Pagebrook, Whig, Sept. 10, 13, 1828, 3
Paine, Capt. Joseph B., Charleston, Enquirer, Aug. 3, 1827, 3
Paine, Mrs. Margaret, Richmond, Enquirer, Oct. 8, 1805, 2
Palmer, Charles, Richmond, Whig, Sept. 2, 1829, 3
Palmer, Dr. Jeffrey D., Meadsville, Whig, Nov. 17, 1835, 2
Palmer, Mrs. Mary Jane, Richmond, Whig, Aug. 13, 1828, 3; Enquirer,
    Aug. 15, 1828, 3
Palmer, William, Middlesex, Whig, Feb. 16, 1838, 4
Pankey, Mrs. Judith S., Cumberland, Enquirer, Feb. 7, 1826, 3
Park, Maj. Robert, Mecklenburg, Whig, Nov. 21, 1837, 2
Parker, George, Northampton, Whig, July 18, 1826, 3; Enquirer, July
    18, 1826, 3
Parker, Col. Josiah, Isle of Wight, Enquirer, March 27, 1810, 3
Parker, Mrs. Margaret T., Gloucester, Enquirer, Aug. 6, 1822, 3
Parker, Mrs. Mary, Westmoreland, Enquirer, Nov. 20, 1810, 3
Parker, Hon. Richard, Westmoreland, Enquirer, April 13, 1813, 3
Parker, Mrs. Roxanna, Richmond, Whig, Oct. 22, 1833, 3
Parker, Col. Thomas, Accomack, Enquirer, Jan. 20, 1820, 3
Parker, Trueman, James City, Whig, Aug. 3, 1832, 3
Parker, William H., Westmoreland, Enquirer, Dec. 16, 1815, 3
Parkinson, Mrs. Nancy, New Kent, Enquirer, Nov. 1, 1822, 3
Parsons, Mrs. Elizabeth, Richmond, Whig, March 24, 1836, 3
Parsons, Samuel, Richmond, Enquirer, March 28, 1820, 3
Parsons, Sarah, Richmond, Whig, March 15, 1828, 3; Enquirer, March 14,
    1828, 3
Partin, Susan, Richmond, Whig, Feb. 2, 1830, 3
Patterson, Edward, Buckingham, Enquirer, June 16, 1826, 3
Patterson, Mrs. Elizabeth W., Northumberland, Enquirer, Nov. 4, 1823, 3

Patterson, John, Mathews, Enquirer, Aug. 13, 1824, 3
Patterson, John B., Mathews, Enquirer, Dec. 7, 1811, 3
Patterson, Thomas, Henrico, Whig, Nov. 21, 1834, 2
Patteson, Alexander, Prince Edward, Whig, Jan. 28, 30, 1836, 3
Patteson, Mrs. Ann, Richmond, Whig, Sept. 1, 1837, 4
Patteson, Charles J., Buckingham, Enquirer, Sept. 2, 5, 1828, 3
Patteson, David, Jr., Manchester, Enquirer, Jan. 2, 1806, 3
Patteson, Mrs. Frances, Lynchburg, Whig, Oct. 13, 1835, 1
Patteson, James Henry, Richmond, Whig, Nov. 20, 1832, 1
Patteson, John, Buckingham, Whig, July 28, 1831, 1
Patteson, Mrs. Mary, Manchester, Whig, Nov. 8, 1833, 1
Patton, Mrs. Ann Gordon, Richmond, Whig, May 16, 1832, 3
Paxton, Mrs. Rebecca Louisa, Rockbridge, Whig, Dec. 19, 1837, 4
Payne, Col. George, Goochland, Whig, May 13, 1831, 4
Payne, George W., Richmond, Whig, Aug. 6, 1833, 3
Payne, Mrs. Jane Beverly, Goochland, Enquirer, July 7, 1826, 3
Payne, Mrs. Lucy, Fluvanna, Enquirer, Dec. 22, 1821, 3
Payne, Mrs. Mary B., Hanover, Enquirer, Feb. 23, 1826, 3
Payne, Samuel, Richmond, Enquirer, May 11, 1821, 3
Payne, Mrs. Sarah, Westmoreland, Enquirer, Aug. 6, 1824, 3
Payne, Mrs. Susan M., Buckingham, Enquirer, April 24, 1821, 3
Peachy, Mrs. Mary Mouro, Williamsburg, Whig, Nov. 26, 1836, 3
Pearce, James A., Richmond, Whig, Dec. 20, 1825, 3
Pearce, Nathaniel C., Manchester, Whig, Aug. 19, 1829, 3
Pearson, Capt. Wm., Richmond, Whig, June 4, 1833, 3
Peck, Alice S., Richmond, Whig, Aug. 24, 1838, 1
Pedigo, Robert, Henry, Enquirer, Jan. 19, 1822, 3
Peers, J. L., Goochland, Enquirer, Nov. 7, 1809, 3
Peers, Thomas, —————, Enquirer, Oct. 22, 1811, 3
Peete, Mrs. Ann, Mecklenburg, Enquirer, Aug. 25, 1826, 3
Pegram, Maj. Edward, Petersburg, Enquirer, Nov. 12, 1814, 3
Pegram, Gen. John, Eastern District, Whig, April 13, 1831, 1
Pegram, Richard G., Dinwiddie, Whig, Nov. 11, 1829, 2
Pemberton, Capt. John B., Henrico, Whig, Sept. 1, 1826, 3
Pemberton, Capt. Thomas, Goochland, Enquirer, Oct. 21, 1828, 3
Pendleton, Amanda Tompkins, Richmond, Whig, Aug. 18, 1831, 1
Pendleton, Edmund, Caroline, Enquirer, July 10, 1827, 3
Pendleton, French Strother, Tazewell Court House, Whig, March 1, 1831, 3
Pendleton, Mrs. Mary Ann, King and Queen, Enquirer, Sept. 29, 1820, 3
Pendleton, Col. Philip, King and Queen, Enquirer, Aug. 8, 1804, 3
Fendleton, Robert C., Caroline, Whig, April 15, 1836, 3
Penn, Col. George, —————, Enquirer, March 25, 1828, 3
Perkins, George, Cumberland, Whig, Oct. 7, 1834, 2
Perkins, Mrs. Mary Senora, Albemarle, Whig, Sept. 9, 1836, 2
Perkins, William H., Buckingham, Enquirer, Dec. 19, 1826, 3
Perkinson, Wm. B., Prince Edward, Whig, Dec. 4, 1835, 1
Perrin, Isaac, Hanover, Enquirer, March 16, 1821, 3
Pescud, Thomas, Warwick, Enquirer, Nov. 17, 1820, 3

Peter, Col. John, Surry, Whig, Jan. 10, 1837, 4
Pettus, Endora Swartwout, Richmond, Whig, June 21, 1836, 3
Pettus, James G., Louisa, Whig, Aug. 10, 1838, 1
Pettus, Mrs. Jane C., Lunenburg, Enquirer, April 11, 1817, 3
Peyton, Cravan, Albemarle, Whig, April 7, 1837, 4
Peyton, Mrs. Eliza S., Stafford, Enquirer, Nov. 1, 1822, 3
Peyton, Mrs. Jane, Albemarle, Enquirer, Dec. 21, 1820, 3
Peyton, Mrs. John R. [Ann], Stafford, Whig, Jan. 10, 1837, 4
Peyton, Mrs. Mary Josephine, Winchester, Enquirer, April 9, 1822, 3
Peyton, Mrs. Sally, Mathews, Enquirer, Oct. 10, 1807, 2
Peyton, Mrs. Susannah, Staunton, Enquirer, July 25, 1820, 3
Phillips, Mrs. Ann, Nelson, Whig, Sept. 15, 1837, 1
Phillips, Hon. John, Richmond, Enquirer, June 10, 1823, 3
Pickett, Charles, Richmond, Enquirer, April 15, 1825, 3
Pickett, George, Richmond, Enquirer, Nov. 20, 1821, 3
Pickett, Margaret, Richmond, Whig, June 1, 1838, 2
Piggott, Mrs. Mary, James City, Enquirer, Feb. 24, 1827, 3
Pilcher, Mrs. Jane, Richmond, Whig, March 21, 1834, 2
Pillsborough, Col. Moses B., Petersburg, Whig, Oct. 2, 1832, 3
Pinchback, Sarah, Richmond, Whig, April 28, 1835, 2
Pindall, James, Clarksburg, Whig, Dec. 16, 1825, 3
Pindall, James, Harrison, Enquirer, Dec. 10, 1825, 3
Pindall, Mrs. Ruhamah, Harrison, Whig, Oct. 10, 1829, 3
Piper, James, Washington, Enquirer, Dec. 16, 1825, 3
Pitkin, Rev. J. B., Richmond, Whig, Feb. 27, 1835, 2
Pitts, Mrs. Ann, Essex, Whig, Nov. 8, 1837, 2
Pitts, David W., Essex, Whig, June 27, 1837, 1, 2
Pitts, Gen. M. S., Northampton, Enquirer, Sept. 25, 1827, 3
Placide, Alexander, Richmond, Whig, March 8, 1836, 1
Pleasants, Ann, Goochland, Enquirer, Sept. 4, 1821, 3
Pleasants, Mrs. Ann Eliza, Lynchburg, Enquirer, May 21, 1819, 3
Pleasants, Archibald, Sr., Goochland, Whig, Aug. 2, 1836, 1
Pleasants, Mrs. Deborah W., Richmond, Whig, May 26, 1837, 2
Pleasants, Mrs. Elizabeth, Richmond, Whig, Sept. 20, 1833, 1
Pleasants, Elizabeth Agnes, Henrico, Enquirer, Nov. 2, 1824, 3
Pleasants, Frederick, Richmond, Enquirer, Oct. 12, 1827, 3
Pleasants, Col. Isaac, Goochland, Whig, Feb. 25, 1825, 3
Pleasants, James, Goochland, Whig, Sept. 28, 1824, 3; Enquirer, Sept.
    28, 1824, 3
Pleasants, James, Goochland, Whig, Nov. 18, 1836, 2
Pleasants, James Madison, —————, Whig, March 26, 1829, 3
Pleasants, Mrs. Jane, Goochland, Enquirer, Feb. 3, 1821, 3
Pleasants, John, Richmond, Whig, Aug. 11, 1829, 3
Pleasants, Mrs. John H. [Mary L.], Richmond, Whig, April 21, 1837, 1
Pleasants, John Woodson, Richmond, Whig, April 1, 1836, 3
Pleasants, Mary C., Henrico, Whig, Jan. 2, 1835, 1
Pleasants, Samuel, —————, Enquirer, Oct. 5, 1814, 3
Pleasants, Mrs. Sarah Maria, Richmond, Enquirer, April 26, 29, 1825, 3
Pleasants, Wm. Henry, Goochland, Whig, Oct. 3, 1826, 3

Pleasants, Dr. Wm. P., Powhatan, Whig, Nov. 1, 1833, 1
Pledge, John W., Richmond, Enquirer, Jan. 27, 1821, 3
Poe, Thomas, Henrico, Whig, Feb. 25, 1825, 3
Poindexter, George, Goochland, Whig, Sept. 30, 1836, 4
Poindexter, Henry Mundy, Richmond, Whig, March 20, 1838, 2
Poindexter, James, Powhatan, Enquirer, April 17, 1816, 3
Poindexter, John Lewis, New Kent, Whig, Dec. 4, 1835, 1
Poindexter, William Green, Goochland, Enquirer, Sept. 24, 1819, 3
Pointer, Samuel, ——————, Enquirer, July 17, 1808, 3
Poitaux, Mrs. Jane, Richmond, Whig, Jan. 3, 1832, 3
Pollard, Elizabeth, Hanover, Enquirer, Nov. 12, 1818, 3
Pollard, Joseph, King and Queen, Whig, Oct. 21, 1836, 4
Pollard, Mary, Lancaster, Enquirer, Feb. 9, 1822, 3
Pollard, Mrs. Mary Ellen, King William, Enquirer, Feb. 26, 1818, 3
Pollard, Mrs. Molly Todd, Hanover, Enquirer, Nov. 19, 1824, 3
Pollard, Richard, King and Queen, Enquirer, Aug. 18, 1809, 3
Pollard, Robert, King William, Enquirer, May 18, 1819, 3
Pollard, Thomas, Hanover, Whig, June 8, 1830, 3
Pollard, Thomas, Halifax, Enquirer, March 27, 1818, 3
Pollok, John, Albemarle, Enquirer, May 2, 1817, 3
Poore, Mrs. Mary, Powhatan, Enquirer, Oct. 14, 1823, 3
Poore, Robert Wm., Richmond, Whig, July 10, 1830, 3
Pope, Alexander, Hanover, Enquirer, Oct. 25, 1808, 3
Pope, Mrs. Anne, Powhatan, Enquirer, Nov. 14, 1823, 3
Pope, Mary Lavina, Goochland, Whig, March 10, 1838, 3
Pope, Capt. Nathaniel, Powhatan, Enquirer, Dec. 2, 1806, 3
Pope, Nathaniel, Hanover, Enquirer, May 23, 1809, 3
Poppal, John, Richmond, Whig, Aug. 11, 1831, 2
Porter, Mrs. Joanna, Powhatan, Enquirer, June 29, 1821, 3
Porter, Mrs. Susan, Chesterfield, Whig, Feb. 19, 1833, 3
Potter, Mrs. Ann, Richmond, Enquirer, March 5, 1811, 3
Potter, Walter, Richmond, Enquirer, Nov. 25, 1817, 3
Potts, John, Manchester, Whig, June 16, 1830, 3
Poultney, Louisa, Lunenburg, Enquirer, June 28, 1825, 3
Povall, Francis B., Powhatan, Whig, July 27, 1838, 2
Povvll [Povall], Dr. Richard, [native of Virginia], Whig, Nov. 8, 1830, 3
Powell, Mrs. Alfred H., Winchester, Enquirer, Oct. 3, 1826, 3
Powell, Alfred Levin, Cartersville, Enquirer, Jan. 31, 1826, 3
Powell, Mrs. Elizabeth, Winchester, Whig, Dec. 9, 16, 1836, 4
Powell, Mrs. Elizabeth, [formerly of Powhatan], Whig, July 11, 1834, 2
Powell, Elizabeth Peyton, Cumberland, Whig, Aug. 16, 1833, 3
Powell, Mrs. Frances, Williamsburg, Enquirer, Oct. 14, 1824, 3
Powell, Ira M., King William, Whig, Sept. 17, 1829, 3
Powell, James and wife, Southampton, Enquirer, June 26, 1821, 2
Powell, John, Gloucester, Enquirer, June 24, 1825, 3
Powell, Leven, Powhatan, Whig, Aug. 16, 1833, 3
Powell, Mrs. Nancy, King William, Enquirer, Aug. 18, 1826, 3
Powell, Wm., King William, Enquirer, June 5, 1822, 3
Powhatan, Wm., Smithfield, Enquirer, Oct. 7, 1823, 3

Poythress, Caroline, Charles City, Enquirer, Oct. 8, 1824, 3
Prentis, Judge Joseph, Richmond, Enquirer, June 23, 1809, 3
Prentiss, Wm., [formerly of Virginia], Whig, Feb. 2, 1831, 3
Prescud, Mrs. Elizabeth, Petersburg, Enquirer, April 16, 1819, 3
Preston, Charles H. C., Abingdon, Whig, Jan. 28, 1832, 3
Preston, Francis, Abingdon, Whig, June 16, 1835, 3
Preston, John, Botetourt, Enquirer, April 10, 1827, 3
Preston, Mrs. John, ————, Enquirer, March 30, 1810, 3
Preston, John, Richmond, Enquirer, April 6, 1827, 3
Preston, Susan, Montgomery, Whig, April 10, 1835, 1
Preston, Thomas L., Lexington, Enquirer, Aug. 18, 1812, 3
Preston, Virginia Ann, Montgomery, Whig, March 5, 1833, 3
Preston, Maj. William, ————, Enquirer, Feb. 10, 13, 1821, 3
Price, Alexander Pope, Petersburg, Enquirer, July 19, 1805, 3
Price, Mrs. E., Goochland, Enquirer, May 4, 1814, 3
Price, Francis R., Henrico, Enquirer, Aug. 30, 1822, 3
Price, John, Henrico, Enquirer, Feb. 24, 1816, 3
Price, John Fleming, Richmond, Enquirer, Feb. 16, 1813, 3
Price, John Lewis, Richmond, Enquirer, Oct. 10, 1806, 3
Price, Mrs. Mary, ————, Enquirer, March 18, 1806, 3
Price, Mrs. Sarah, Richmond, Whig, Jan. 27, 1837, 3
Price, Mrs. Sarbara, Hanover, Whig, June 9, 1831, 4
Price, Mrs. Susannah W., Henrico, Whig, Aug. 19, 1825, 3
Price, Capt. Thomas, Hanover, Whig, Jan. 3, 1837, 2
Price, Thomas, Sr., Hanover, Whig, Dec. 16, 1836, 2
Price, William, Buckingham, Enquirer, Oct. 18, 1808, 3
Price, Maj. Wm., Richmond, Whig, June 29, 1830, 3
Price, William, Buckingham, Enquirer, Oct. 18, 1808, 3
Prichard, Mrs. Ann, Richmond, Whig, Sept. 22, 1831, 1
Priddy, Thomas, Richmond, Whig, Jan. 6, 1832, 1
Pride, Thomas R., Amelia, Enquirer, Feb. 24, 1821, 3
Primrose, Mrs. Rebecca, Richmond, Whig, Feb. 4, 1832, 1
Primrose, Robert L., Amelia, Enquirer, March 18, 1823, 3
Pritchard, William, Richmond, Enquirer, March 4, 1815, 3
Pritchett, Elizabeth G., Orange, Whig, Jan. 16, 1838, 1
Probst, Mrs. Elizabeth, Richmond, Whig, Sept. 28, 1832, 1
Proctor, Francis, Richmond, Whig, Jan. 2, 1835, 1
Prosser, Albert Henry, Wilkinson, Enquirer, Dec. 23, 1826, 3
Prosser, John, Richmond, Enquirer, Oct. 30, 1810, 3
Prosser, Letitia, Henrico, Enquirer, March 14, 1817, 3
Prosser, Mrs. Lucy B., [formerly of Richmond], Enquirer, Oct. 25, 1822, 3
Prosser, Wm. H., Gloucester, Whig, Oct. 3, 1827, 3; Enquirer, Oct. 9, 1827, 3
Prunty, Capt. John, Clarksburg, Enquirer, April 15, 1823, 3
Pryor, Gen, Brazure W., Norfolk, Whig, April 27, 1827, 3; Enquirer, April 20, 1827, 3
Pryor, Mrs. Elizabeth A., Elizabeth City, Whig, Dec. 28, 1824, 3; Enquirer, Dec. 21, 1824, 3
Pryor, Maj. John, Richmond, Enquirer, March 25, 1823, 3

Puckett, Mrs. Susan B., Richmond, Whig, Nov. 19, 1829, 3
Puckett, Wm. T., Richmond, Enquirer, Oct. 26, 1827, 3
Pugh, Mrs. Judith, Richmond, Whig, Jan. 13, 1826, 3,
Puller, Mrs. Elizabeth, King William, Enquirer, Jan. 6, 1824, 4
Puller, William D., King William, Enquirer, Sept. 28, 1827, 3
Pulliam, Mrs. Sally, Henrico, Whig, May 23, 1837, 3
Pulliam, Mrs. Samuel T. [Clara Waller], Richmond, Whig, Feb. 3, 1837, 3
Pulling, Thomas, Richmond, Whig, Sept. 21, 1829, 3
Pully, George Edwin, Mecklenburg, Whig, July 8, 1836, 3
Puryear, Mrs. Ann, Goochland, Enquirer, Nov. 15, 1815, 3
Puryear, Smith, Richmond, Whig, July 21, 1831, 3
Puryear, Thomas, Goochland, Enquirer, July 2, 1813, 1
Pyle, Rachel, Richmond, Whig, June 15, 1832, 3

Q.

Quarles, Mrs. Elizabeth, King William, Enquirer, July 3, 1810, 3
Quarles, Col. James, Goochland, Enquirer, June 1, 1824, 3
Quarles, Maj. John, Fluvanna, Enquirer, July 31, 1816, 3
Quarles, John, Spottsylvania, Enquirer, May 22, 25, 1821, 3
Quarles, Mrs. Lucy Daingerfield, Enquirer, Feb. 15, 1820, 3
Quarles, Mrs. Mary, Fluvanna, Enquirer, Dec. 10, 1816, 3
Quarles, Dr. Pryor, ————, Enquirer, Oct. 16, 1821, 3
Quarles, William, King William, Whig, Sept. 1, 1837, 4
Quesenberry, Wm. S., Caroline, Whig, Nov. 11, 1834, 4

R.

Raban, George, Richmond, Whig, Nov. 26, 1828, 4
Radford, George, Powhatan, Enquirer, Dec. 1, 1820, 3
Ragland, Dr. John C., Charlottesville, Enquirer, Jan. 6, 1824, 3
Ragland, Shelton, Hanover, Whig, Dec. 2, 1825, 3
Ragland, Mrs. Shelton, Hanover, Whig, Dec. 2, 1825, 3
Raine, John, Cumberland, Enquirer, May 24, 1815, 3
Ralston, Mrs. Janet, Richmond, Whig, July 29, 1834, 1
Ralston, Janet Elizabeth, Lexington, Whig, Sept. 23, 1836, 4
Randolph, Mrs. Ann, Henrico, Enquirer, Feb. 23, 1828, 3
Randolph, Mrs. Ann, Powhatan, Enquirer, Jan. 25, 1820, 3
Randolph, Anne Valentine, Goochland, Whig, Jan. 26, 1838, 4
Randolph, Capt. Archibald, Frederick, Enquirer, Nov. 30, 1813, 3
Randolph, Brett, Henrico, Whig, March 1, 1828, 3; Enquirer, Feb. 26, 1828, 3
Randolph, Brett N., Powhatan, Enquirer, Oct. 5, 1819, 3
Randolph, Mrs. Caroline Matilda, Warwick, Enquirer, Sept. 30, 1808, 3
Randolph, David Meade, Norfolk, Enquirer, Oct. 18, 1825, 3
Randolph, David Meade, Richmond, Whig, Oct. 4, 1830, 3
Randolph, Edwin, Richmond, Whig, Sept. 10, 1833, 1
Randolph, Mrs. Elizabeth, Richmond, Enquirer, March 9, 1810, 3
Randolph, Mrs. Harriet, Tuckahoe, Enquirer, Feb. 5, 1822, 3

Randolph, Dr. John, Amelia, Whig, July 29, 1834, 2
Randolph, John, Roanoke, Whig, June 4, 1833, 2
Randolph, Mrs. Judith, Richmond, Enquirer, March 13, 1816, 3
Randolph, Louisa Gabriella, Chesterfield, Whig, Jan. 26, 1838, 4
Randolph, Mrs. Maria, Richmond, Whig, March 22, 25, 1825, 3; April 1, 12, 1825, 3
Randolph, Mrs. Mary, ――――, Enquirer, Jan. 29, 1828, 3
Randolph, Mrs. Mary R., "Morven," Enquirer, April 22, 1806, 3
Randolph, Peyton, Richmond, Whig, Dec. 29, 1828, 3
Randolph, Robert, Fauquier, Enquirer, Sept. 27, 1825, 3
Randolph, Robert Levingston, Tuckahoe, Whig, Aug. 22, 1831, 4
Randolph, Mrs. Sarah, Henrico, Enquirer, April 16, 1819, 3
Randolph, Col. Thomas Mann, Albemarle, Whig, June 25, 1828, 3; Enquirer, June 27, 1828, 3
Rankins, Catharine, Port Royal, Whig, Oct. 29, 1833, 1
Ransome, Robert, Gloucester, Enquirer, June 22, 1819, 3
Ravenscroft, Mrs. Ann, Lunenburg, Enquirer, Aug. 23, 1815, 3
Rawleigh, William, Richmond, Enquirer, June 14, 1811, 3
Rawlings, Wm. P., Petersburg, Enquirer, Oct. 1, 1813, 3
Rawlins, Elizabeth Marion, Richmond, Whig, May 15, 1835, 4
Rawlins, Mrs. Sarah, Caroline, Enquirer, Jan. 20, 1824, 3
Read, Horace, Richmond, Whig, Aug. 30, 1833, 3
Read, Isaac, Charlotte, Enquirer, July 18, 1823, 3
Read, Dr. John K., Goochland, Enquirer, March 5, 1805, 3
Read, Samuel V., Charlotte, Enquirer, Sept. 29, 1820, 3
Reardon, Matthew, Norfolk, Enquirer, Oct. 5, 1827, 3
Reat, James, Richmond, Enquirer, Feb. 25, 1815, 3
Redd, George W., Prince Edward, Enquirer, Jan. 2, 1813, 3
Redd, Col. James M., Patrick, Whig, July 28, 1837, 4
Redd, Mrs. Keziah, Henry, Enquirer, Aug. 11, 1818, 3
Redford, Marcella, Goochland, Whig, March 9, 1832, 3
Redford, Richard, Goochland, Enquirer, Jan. 13, 18, 1823, 3
Redford, Wm. C., Manchester, Whig, Oct. 9, 1835, 4
Redford, Worthington Augustus, Goochland, Whig, Nov. 10, 1835, 2
Redwood, John, New Kent, Enquirer, Feb. 18, 1826, 3
Reed, Warren, Richmond, Whig, July 10, 1838, 1
Reeve, Hon. Tapping, ――――, Enquirer, Dec. 27, 1823, 3
Reid, ――――, ――――, Whig, Nov. 24, 1830, 3
Reid, Andrew, Richmond, Whig, Oct. 17, 1837, 4
Reid, Andrew, Nelson, Enquirer, Sept. 12, 13, 1811, 3
Reid, Maj. John, Bedford, Enquirer, Feb. 3, 1816, 3
Rennolds, Streshly, Essex, Enquirer, Aug. 6, 1822, 3
Renyon, William, ――――, Enquirer, Jan. 27, 1827, 3
Revell, Mrs. Edward A. [Catharine], Accomack, Whig, Feb. 21, 1837, 4
Reverley, George, Campbell, Enquirer, Dec. 31, 1822, 3
Reverley, Harriot, Campbell, Enquirer, Dec. 17, 1822, 3
Reves, Henry, Buckingham, Enquirer, Oct. 26, 1824, 3
Reynolds, David H., Richmond, Whig, Oct. 25, 1836, 1
Reynolds, Mrs. Sarah, Richmond, Whig, Sept. 9, 1830, 3

Rice, Rev. Dr., ——————, Whig, Sept. 12, 1831, 4
Richards, Jonathan, Richmond, Enquirer, Feb. 9, 1819, 3
Richards, Mrs. Susan E. W., Richmond, Whig, Dec. 21, 1832, 3
Richardson, Mrs. Ann, Lynchburg, Enquirer, March 15, 1822, 3
Richardson, Eleanor, Fredericksburg, Enquirer, Aug. 14, 1821, 3
Richardson, Maj. George, Richmond. Enquirer, Oct. 18, 1805, 3
Richardson, James G., Richmond, Whig, June 3, 1830, 3
Richardson, John, Richmond, Whig, July 9, 1833, 3
Richardson, John, New Kent, Enquirer, Dec. 18, 1813, 3
Richardson, Mrs. Martha, Hanover, Whig, Oct. 4, 1828, 3; Enquirer, Oct.
    3, 1828, 3
Richardson, Martha Ann, Richmond, Enquirer, March 23, 1827, 3
Richardson, Martin W., [formerly of Cumberland], Enquirer, Oct. 17,
    1826, 3
Richardson, Nathaniel B., Richmond, Enquirer, July 26, 1822, 3
Richardson, Col. Samuel, Fluvanna, Enquirer, Appril 7, 1807, 3
Richardson, Samuel, Hanover, Enquirer, June 16, 1820, 3
Richardson, Thomas, Richmond, Whig, Dec. 19, 1831, 3
Richardson, Capt. William, Richmond, Enquirer, June 13, 1809, 3
Richardson, William T., Richmond, Enquirer, Sept. 14, 1816, 3
Riddick, Mrs. Anna Maria, Rocky Mills, Enquirer, Aug. 29, 1804, 3
Riddick, Lemuel, Hanover, Whig, Oct. 3, 1826, 3
Riddle, James D., Richmond, Enquirer, Feb. 15, 1825, 3
Riddle, John A., Matthews, Enquirer, Aug. 5, 1823, 3
Ritchie, Archibald, Essex, Enquirer, May 30, 1828, 3
Ritchie, George, Richmond, Whig, Nov. 3, 1835, 1
Rivalain, Lewis M., Richmond, Whig, Oct. 14, 1825, 3
Rives, Mrs. Margaret, Nelson, Enquirer, Aug. 30, 1815, 3
Roane, Charlotte N., King and Queen, Enquirer, Nov. 1, 1815, 3
Roane, Mrs. Elizabeth, King and Queen, Whig, Nov. 25, 1825, 3; En-
    quirer, Nov. 22, 1825, 3
Roane, John, Jr., King and Queen, Enquirer, April 24, 1810, 3
Roane, John, Middlesex, Enquirer, Dec. 6, 1810, 3
Roane, Mrs. Martha [Selden], ——————, Enquirer, Aug. 14, 17, 1810, 3
Roane, Martha Ann, Charles City, Whig, Nov. 17, 1826, 3
Roane, Mrs. Mary, Amherst, Whig, Oct. 17, 1829, 3
Roane, Newman B., King William, Enquirer, April 15, 1825, 3
Roane, Patrick H., Richmond, Enquirer, Feb. 3, 1814, 3
Roane, Samuel, King and Queen, Enquirer, Feb. 27, 1807, 3
Roane, Mrs. Sarah A., Richmond, Whig, April 30, 1828, 3; Enquirer,
    April 29, 1828, 3
Roane, Spencer, Bath, Enquirer, Sept. 13, 17, 1822, 3
Roane, Thomas, King and Queen, Enquirer, Jan. 23, 1808, 3
Robbins, Mrs. Martha H., Richmond, Whig, Dec. 8, 1835, 4
Roberson, Mrs. Francis C., Halifax, Enquirer, Nov. 13, 1821, 3
Roberts, James, ——————, Enquirer, March 16, 1814, 2
Roberts, Mrs. Mary, New Kent, Whig, March 10, 1857, 4
Roberts, Col. Thomas, Winchester, Whig, May 30, 1837, 2
Roberts, Thomas, Buckingham, Enquirer, Feb. 10, 1814, 3

Robertson, Mrs. Ann B., Kanawha, Enquirer, Sept. 16, 1823, 3
Robertson, Arthur, Bedford, Enquirer, Nov. 6, 1821, 3
Robertson, David, Petersburg, Enquirer, June 17, 1823, 3
Robertson, Elizabeth Jane, Richmond, Enquirer, Aug. 16, 1822, 3
Robertson, Mrs. Elizabeth M., Richmond, Enquirer, Nov. 25, 1823, 3
Robertson, James, Amelia, Enquirer, Sept. 26, 1828, 3
Robertson, Mrs. Jane, Petersburg, Enquirer, Jan. 31, 1824, 3
Robertson, Jeffrey, Buckingham, Enquirer, April 17, 1827, 3
Robertson, John, Amelia, Enquirer, March 7, 1826, 3
Robertson, John, Richmond, Whig, Aug. 13, 1828, 3
Robertson, Dr. John, Petersburg, Whig, Jan. 24, 1832, 1
Robertson, John, Culpeper, Enquirer, Oct. 20, 1818, 3
Robertson, Mrs. Mary E., Amelia, Enquirer, May 1, 1818, 3
Robertson, Philemon Holcombe, Richmond, Whig, Aug. 26, 1825, 3; Enquirer, Aug. 16, 1825, 3
Robertson, Powhatan, ————, Enquirer, Nov. 28, 1820, 3
Robertson, Rebecca, Richmond, Enquirer, March 4, 1823, 3
Robertson, Mrs. Tabitha, Powhatan, Enquirer, Feb. 27, 1827, 3
Robertson, Wm., Richmond, Whig, Nov. 19, 1829, 3
Robinson, Mrs. Adaline, Petersburg, Whig, April 3, 1825, 3
Robinson, Alexander L., Richmond, Whig, Oct. 13, 1831, 2
Robinson, Benjamin, Spottsylvania, Enquirer, Feb. 20, 1821, 3
Robinson, James C., King and Queen, Enquirer, Sept. 11, 1821, 3
Robinson, John, Rockbridge, Whig, July 18, 1826, 3; Enquirer, July 25, 1826, 3
Robinson, John, Lexington, Enquirer, July 25, 1826, 3
Robinson, Mary Skipwith, Powhatan, Whig, Aug. 8, 1834, 2
Robinson, Merritt M., Richmond, Whig, July 23, 1828, 3; Enquirer, July 25, 1828, 3
Robinson, Wm., Richmond, Whig, Jan. 28, 1832, 3
Rodgers, John, Westmoreland, Enquirer, Nov. 13, 1813, 3
Roffe, Melchezidick, Mecklenburg, Enquirer, May 11, 1827, 3
Rogers, John, Albemarle, Whig, May 22, 1838, 1
Rogers, Dr. Patrick K., Ellicott's Mills, Whig, Aug. 9, 1828, 3; Enquirer, Aug. 12, 1828, 3
Rootes, Thomas R., Gloucester, Enquirer, Jan. 15, 1824, 3
Roper, Rev. David, Richmond, Whig, March 6, 1827, 3; Enquirer, March 10, 1828, 3
Roper, Edmund P., Richmond, Whig, Jan. 5, 1835, 1
Roper, Edward, Charles City, Enquirer, March 14, 1826, 3
Roper, Mrs. Sarah W., Richmond, Whig, Aug. 10, 1932, 3
Roper, Mrs. Susan, Richmond, Whig, March 22, 1828, 3
Rose, Capt. Alexander Fontaine, Stafford, Whig, Dec. 2, 1831, 3
Rose, George Nicholas, Amherst, Whig, May 16, 1837, 2
Rose, James, Richmond, Whig, Feb. 11, 1832, 3
Rose, Dr. Robert Henry, ————, Whig, Sept. 13, 1833, 1
Rose, Hon. Robert Selden, Amherst, Whig, Dec. 8, 1835, 3
Rose, Thomas, Dinwiddie, Whig, March 26, 1829, 3
Rose, William, Richmond, Whig, Feb. 19, 1830, 3

Rose, William, Richmond, Enquirer, July 8, 1817, 3
Roskins, John, King William, Enquirer, Nov. 21, 1820, 3
Ross, John, Richmond, Whig, Oct. 6, 1837, 2
Ross, William, Mt. Ida, Enquirer, Sept. 26, 1804, 3
Rouzee, Mrs. Elizabeth, Powhatan, Whig, Oct. 13, 1835, 1
Row, Maj. James G., King and Queen, Enquirer, Jan. 22, 1822, 3
Row, Lucy A., King and Queen, Whig, April 12, 1825, 3
Rowland, Margaret H., Richmond, Whig, June 13, 1834, 2
Rowlett, George H., Richmond, Whig, June 16, 1837, 1
Rowlett, John, Richmond, Whig, Sept. 23, 1834, 4
Rowlett, Wm., Jr., Richmond, Whig, June 11, 1833, 3
Roy, Mrs. Ann, Mathews, Whig, Sept. 19, 1834, 2
Roy, John, Caroline, Whig, May 16, 1834, 2
Roy, Dr. Wiley, King and Queen, Enquirer, Nov. 7, 1817, 3
Royal, William, Lynchburg, Enquirer, July 1, 1817, 3
Royall, John Albert, Manchester, Whig, Jan. 23, 1838, 2
Royall, Wm., Charles City, Enquirer, June 17, 1828, 3
Royster, James H., Richmond, Whig, May 24, 1833, 1
Royster, Mrs. Jane, Richmond, Whig, April 4, 1834, 3
Royster, John, Goochland, Whig, June 22, 1832, 3
Royster, John H., Richmond, Enquirer, Feb. 4, 1816, 3
Royster, Dr. Joseph R., Goochland, Enquirer, April 18, 1826, 3
Rudd, James J., Hanover, Enquirer, March 7, 1826, 3
Ruffin, Sterling, ————, Enquirer, May 14, 1822, 3
Ruffin, Dr. Thomas, ————, Enquirer, Sept. 13, 1822, 3
Ruggles, Timothy, ————, Enquirer, July 22, 1825, 3
Russell, Mrs. Sarah A., ————, Enquirer, July 29, 1828, 3
Russell, Armistead, Richmond, Whig, Aug. 7, 1832, 1
Russell, Maj. John, [formerly of Hanover], Enquirer, Jan. 23, 1821, 3
Russell, William, Williamsburg, Enquirer, April 28, 1812, 3
Rust, Mary Frances, Richmond, Whig, May 28, 1829, 3
Rust, Sarah Ann, Richmond, Whig, Jan. 20, 1837, 2
Ryland, Mrs. Elizabeth, King William, Enquirer, June 9, 1826, 3
Ryland, John Hollins, ————, Whig, Jan. 19, 1838, 3

S.

Sackrider, Mrs. Mary, Richmond, Enquirer, Aug. 17, 1810, 3
Salle, Mrs. Sarah, Manchester, Whig, Jan. 27, 1829, 3
Sample, Andrew, Franklin, Whig, Dec. 10, 1824, 3; Enquirer, Dec. 3, 1824, 3
Sampson, Mrs. Eliza, Powhatan, Enquirer, Aug. 21, 1827, 3
Sampson, James Epperson, Richmond, Whig, Aug. 11, 1831, 4
Sampson, Leslie Watson, Cumberland, Whig, July 8, 1834, 3
Sampson, Robert, Goochland, Whig, Sept. 3, 1828, 3; Enquirer, Sept. 5, 1828, 3
Sanders, Mildred, Goochland, Whig, April 10, 1830, 3
Sandidge, Mrs. Ann, Spottsylvania, Whig, Feb. 11, 1825, 3
Sandidge, Mrs. Elizabeth N., Richmond, Whig, Nov. 21, 1837, 4

Sands, Mary Ellen, Goochland, Whig, May 11, 1831, 3
Sangster, Maj. James, Fairfax, Whig, Oct. 25, 1836, 1
Satith, Granville, ——————, Enquirer, Nov. 18, 1825, 3
Saunders, Archer Dennis, James City, Whig, March 5, 1832, 3
Saunders, Mrs. Elizabeth, Goochland, Whig, Oct. 30, 1832, 1
Saunders, George, King and Queen, Whig, Feb. 11, 1831, 3
Saunders, George, King and Queen, Enquirer, July 18, 1820, 3
Saunders, Mrs. G. A. [Frances], Richmond, Whig, Feb. 21, 1837, 4
Saunders, Mrs. Hannah, Powhatan, Whig, Aug. 15, 1834, 1
Saunders, Hetty Fleming, New Kent, Whig, Sept. 17, 1828, 3; Enquirer,
    Oct. 7, 1828, 3
Saunders, Maj. John, ——————, Enquirer, April 6, 1810, 2
Saunders, John H., Powhatan, Enquirer, July 25, 1817, 3
Saunders, Mrs. Marianne, Williamsburg, Enquirer, Dec. 28, 1809, 3
Saunders, Mrs. Mary, Goochland, Enquirer, Feb. 10, 1809, 3
Saunders, Mrs. Mary P., Richmond, Whig, July 8, 1836, 1
Saunders, Robert Fleming, Henrico, Whig, Jan. 28, 1836, 1
Saunders, Col. Robert H., Henrico, Whig, Oct. 8, 1833, 1
Saunders, Tarlton, Richmond, Whig, June 9, 1831, 4
Savage, George, Henrico, Enquirer, June 4, 1824, 3
Savage, Nancy, New Kent, Whig, Oct. 13, 1835, 1
Savage, Mrs. Sarah, Accomac, Enquirer, July 25, 1826, 3
Savage, Willie T., Surry, Whig, Jan. 31, 1837, 3
Saval, Col. Jacinth, Harper's Ferry, Enquirer, Sept. 13, 1822, 3
Sawyers, Helen Christiana, Richmond, Whig, Aug. 26, 1825, 3
Sayre, Mrs. Virginia, Middlesex, Enquirer, May 25, 1821, 3
Scea, Mrs. Campbell, Whig, Aug. 9, 1828, 3
Schaeffer, Rev. Frederick, Richmond, Whig, April 1, 1831, 3
Schenk, Catharine E., Hanover, Whig, Dec. 28, 1824, 3
Schenk, Catharine E., Louisa, Enquirer, Dec. 21, 1824, 3
Schermerhorn, Mrs. Sarah Christian, ——————, Enquirer, May 21,
    1822, 3
Scott, Catharine T., Halifax, Enquirer, April 26, 1825, 3
Scott, Capt. Charles, Halifax, Enquirer, March 23, 1819, 3
Scott, Edward Winfield, near Richmond, Whig, May 18, 1827, 3
Scott, Isabella, Manchester, Whig, Oct. 7, 1834, 2
Scott, James B., Manchester, Whig, June 18, 1833, 3
Scott, Dr. John, Albemarle, Whig, Sept. 7, 1829, 3
Scott, John, Caroline, Enquirer, Feb. 28, 1822, 3
Scott, John, Powhatan, Enquirer, Dec. 25, 1821, 3
Scott, Maj. Joseph, ——————, Enquirer, Dec. 4, 8, 1810, 3
Scott, Mrs. Lucy, Amelia, Enquirer, March 10, 1818, 3
Scott, Mrs. Martha C., Richmond, Enquirer, May 7, 1814, 3
Scott, Mrs. Mary, Campbell, Enquirer, Oct. 9, 1827, 3
Scott, Mrs. Mary Coles, Halifax, Enquirer, Aug. 28, 1810, 3
Scott, Mrs. Patcy, Caroline, Enquirer, Jan. 26, 1813, 3
Scott, Mrs. Richard M., Fairfax, Enquirer, Jan. 14, 30, 1812, 3
Scott, Capt. Thomas, Amelia, Enquirer, July 19, 1825, 3
Scott, Wm., Norfolk, Enquirer, Aug. 3, 1814, 4

Scully, Barnaby, Petersburg, Enquirer, April 26, 1825, 3
Seaman, John, —————, Enquirer, Oct. 16, 1816, 3
Seaton, John, —————, Enquirer, July 17, 1808, 3
Seaton, Wm., Richmond, Enquirer, Sept. 26, 1826, 3
Seay, Efford Booker, Amelia, Enquirer, Oct. 24, 1823, 3
Seay, Mrs. Rebecca M., Columbia, Enquirer, Sept. 17, 1822, 3
Seddon, Thomas, Fredericksburg, Whig, Aug. 18, 1831, 1
Seeds, Robert, King and Queen, Aug. 13, 1822, 3
Seeds, Dr. Thomas, King and Queen, Enquirer, Aug. 6, 1822, 3
Segar, Mrs. Sarah G., Northampton, Whig, June 4, 1833, 3
Selden, Mrs. Betty, Richmond, Whig, April 11, 1834, 1
Selden, Cary, Stafford, Enquirer, Dec. 14, 1822, 3
Selden, Charles Douglas, Amelia, Whig, Sept. 15, 1837, 1
Selden, Mrs. Eliza Maria, Richmond, Whig, Oct. 28, 1834, 4
Selden, Joseph, —————, Enquirer, Jan. 31, 1807, 3
Selden, Col. Miles, Prince George, Enquirer, May 21, 1814, 3
Selden, Col. Miles, Henrico, Enquirer, May 24, 1811, 3
Selden, Mrs. Nathaniel, Henrico, Enquirer, June 28, 1811, 3
Selden, Richard, Lancaster, Enquirer, Dec. 20, 1823, 3
Selden, Dr. Wilson Carey, Leesburg, Whig, April 7, 1835, 2
Selden, Mrs. Sarah A., Charles City, Whig, Sept. 22, 1837, 2
Semon, Peter, Williamsburg, Enquirer, March 11, 1817, 3
Semple, George, Hanover, Enquirer, Feb. 8, 1821, 3
Semple, George T., Franklin, Enquirer, Feb. 22, 1825, 3
Semple, Mrs. Johannah, Williamsburg, Enquirer, July 6, 1824, 3
Semple, John, King and Queen, Enquirer, May 31, 1822, 3
Semple, Robert B., Fredericksburg, Whig, Jan. 3, 1832, 1
Shackelford, Edmund, [native of Virginia], Whig, May 31, 1833, 1
Shackelford, John W., Albemarle, Whig, Dec. 9, 1836, 4
Shackelford, Lyne, —————, Enquirer, May 20, 1806, 3
Shackelford, William, Richmond, Whig, May 31, 1833, 1
Shapard, Robert, Richmond, Whig, Jan. 1, 1829, 3
Sharp, Col. William, Norfolk, Enquirer, Sept. 16, 1823, 3
Shaub, John, —————, Enquirer, Jan. 4, 1812, 3
Shaw, Mrs. Martha Ann, Richmond, Whig, Nov. 28, 1834, 4
Shearman, William, Orange, Enquirer, Oct. 5, 1824, 3
Sheen, George, Chesterfield, Whig, May 5, 1835, 3
Sheffy, Daniel, near Warm Springs, Whig, Dec. 9, 1830, 3
Shelton, Harriet Ellen, [near Bowling Green], Whig, Oct. 4, 1833, 1
Shelton, John, Suffolk, Enquirer, Jan. 20, 1821, 4
Shelton, Mrs. Nancy, Richmond, Whig, Aug. 22, 1826, 3
Shelton, Philip Turner, Hanover, Enquirer, March 1, 1821, 3
Shelton, Richard I., Danville, Whig, Jan. 28, 1831, 3
Shelton, Capt. Wm. A., Goochland, Enquirer, Jan. 15, 1824, 3
Shepard, Mrs. Mary, Richmond, Whig, Dec. 12, 1834, 3
Shepherd, Andrew T., Richmond, Whig, Oct. 5, 1832, 2
Shepherd, Mrs. Mary, Fluvanna, Enquirer, July 22, 1815, 3
Shepherd, Sarah Terrell, Fluvanna, Whig, March 8, 1838, 4
Sheppard, Capt. Benjamin, Richmond, Whig, Oct. 23, 1832, 1

Sheppard, Elizabeth Smelt, Richmond, Whig, May 5, 1837, 2
Sheppard, Eusebia M., Richmond, Whig, Feb. 28, 1832, 4
Sheppard, Mary S., Richmond, Whig, Dec. 29, 1826, 3; Enquirer, Dec. 27, 1826, 3
Sheppard, Mosby, Henrico, Whig, Feb. 2, 1831, 3
Sheppard, Nathaniel, Richmond, Enquirer, April 29, 1828, 3; Whig, 30, 1828, 3
Sheppard, Mrs. Sarah, Hanover, Enquirer, Dec. 30, 1823, 3
Sheppard, Mrs. S. A., Henrico, Whig, Dec. 22, 1831, 3
Sherman, William, Orange, Enquirer, Oct. 5, 1824, 3
Sherrard, Col. John, Morgan, Whig, April 11, 1837, 2
Shield, Henry Howard, Elizabeth City, Whig, Dec. 28, 1824, 3
Shield, Capt. Samuel, York, Enquirer, May 7, 1814, 3
Shields, Maj. David, Cumberland, Whig, Sept. 5, 1837, 2
Shields, Capt. John P., Richmond, Whig, May 22, 1827, 3
Shields, Mrs. Mary, Richmond, Whig, Sept. 17, 1833, 4
Shields, Mrs. Phebe, Rockbridge, Enquirer, Feb. 7, 1809, 3
Shore, John, Petersburg, Enquirer, May 29, 1813, 2
Shudi, Mrs. Christiana, Richmond, Enquirer, June 3, 1828, 3
Simkins, Wm. J., Northampton, Enquirer, March 11, 1828, 3; Whig, March 12, 1828, 3
Simms, Col. Charles, Alexander, Enquirer, Sept. 7, 1819, 3
Simpson, James, Surry, Enquirer, Dec. 11, 1823, 3
Simpson, Mrs. Mary Caroline, Brunswick, Enquirer, July 27, 1827, 3
Sims, Mrs. Polly Langhorne, Buckingham, Whig, Dec. 30, 1836, 4
Sinclair, Mrs. Margaret Ann, Gloucester, Whig, Sept. 26, 1837, 2
Singleton, Gen. James, Winchester, Enquirer, March 1, 1815, 3
Singleton, Peter, Norfolk, Whig, Jan. 5, 1838, 1
Sinton, Elizabeth G., Richmond, Whig, June 22, 1838, 2
Sizer, Sarah Frances, Caroline, Whig, May 14, 1833, 1
Sizer, William, Powhatan, Whig, March 11, 1825, 3
Skelton, Dr. E. W., Powhatan, Whig, Nov. 11, 1836, 2
Skipwith, Henry, Powhatan, Enquirer, Sept. 27, 1815, 3
Skurry, John, Amelia, Enquirer, March 20, 1818, 3
Slater, John, Richmond, Whig, Jan. 19, 1838, 1
Slater, Meredith, New Kent, Whig, Oct. 17, 1837, 4
Slaughter, Mrs. Catherine, Jefferson, Enquirer, Jan. 15, 1822, 3
Slaughter, Catharine, Lexington, Enquirer, June 14, 1811, 3
Slaughter, Dr. Charles, Charlotte, Enquirer, Oct. 11, 1825, 3
Slaughter, Mrs. Letitia, Culpeper, Enquirer, Feb. 23, 1828, 3
Slaughter, Martin, Culpeper, Whig, Dec. 22, 1835, 3
Sledd, John, Louisa, Enquirer, July 13, 1827, 3
Sledge, Mrs. Mary, Cabin Point, Enquirer, Aug. 14, 1827, 3
Smart, Mrs. Louisa, Gloucester, Enquirer, Oct. 25, 1828, 3
Smith, Aarone, Charlotte Court House, Enquirer, Feb. 24, 1827, 3
Smith, Mrs. Ann, Richmond, Whig, Aug. 18, 1837, 3
Smith, Mrs. Ann C., Richmond, Whig, Aug. 2, 1836, 1
Smith, Catharine, Richmond, Enquirer, Jan. 5, 1821, 3
Smith, Charles, Louisa, Enquirer, Oct. 14, 1815, 3

Smith, Edward, Winchester, Enquirer, Jan. 2, 1827, 3
Smith, Eliza, Gloucester, Enquirer, Jan. 18, 1821, 3
Smith, Mrs. Elizabeth, Chesterfield, Enquirer, July 24, 1816, 3
Smith, Mrs. Ellice M., Richmond, Whig, Nov. 8, 1837, 4
Smith, Francis Linnaeus, Williamsburg, Whig, Feb. 4, 1832, 3
Smith, George Loyall, Richmond, Whig, March 20, 1832, 3
Smith, Gov. George William, Richmond, Enquirer, Jan. 4, 1812, 3
Smith, Geo. Wm., Westmoreland, Enquirer, Oct. 14, 1823, 3
Smith, Granville, Goochland, Enquirer, Nov. 18, 1825, 3
Smith, Granville, Richmond, Whig, Jan. 10, 1826, 3
Smith, Harriet Lucretia, —————, Enquirer, May 16, 1823, 3
Smith, Jacob, Henrico, Whig, July 14, 1830, 3
Smith, Jacob Payne, Henrico, Whig, May 2, 1834, 2
Smith, James, Goochland, Whig, Nov. 25, 1825, 3
Smith, James Graham, Richmond, Enquirer, Feb. 8, 1821, 3
Smith, Jesse, Henrico, Enquirer, June 19, 1821, 3
Smith, Gen. John, Westmoreland, Whig, March 12, 1836, 3
Smith, Dr. John, King and Queen, Enquirer, Dec. 22, 1807, 3
Smith, John D., Richmond, Whig, Nov. 20, 1832, 2
Smith, John P., Richmond, Whig, Sept. 1, 1831, 1
Smith, John Snelson, Louisa, Whig, July 18, 1837, 1
Smith, Col. Larkin, Fredericksburg, Enquirer, Oct. 8, 1813, 3
Smith, Lysander, Powhatan, Whig, Oct. 4, 1830, 3
Smith, Marcellus, Goochland, Whig, Feb. 24, 1829, 3
Smith, Maria, Richmond, Whig, March 26, 1832, 3
Smith, Mary Ann, Richmond, Whig, Oct. 10, 1837, 2
Smith, Rev. Pero G., —————, Enquirer, July 31, 1807, 3
Smith, Philip Armistead, Mathews, Enquirer, Nov. 2, 1813, 3
Smith, Reuben, Pohite, Enquirer, Sept. 22, 1820, 3
Smith, Richard, Richmond, Enquirer, June 23, 1809, 3
Smith, Robert K., Richmond, Whig, Feb. 25, 1825, 3
Smith, Mrs. Sarah, Richmond, Enquirer, Oct. 7, 1806, 3
Smith, Mrs. Sarah Ann, Richmond, Whig, Dec. 16, 1836, 3
Smith, Mrs. Sarah G., Louisa, Enquirer, May 24, 1811, 3
Smith, Rev. Sterling, —————, Enquirer, Sept. 26, 1828, 3
Smith, Mrs. Susanna, King and Queen, Enquirer, Oct. 3, 1826, 3
Smith, Susannah Drinker, Richmond, Whig, June 19, 1838, 2
Smith, Mrs. Tabitha, Louisa, Enquirer, Dec. 3, 1819, 3
Smith, Thomas, Essex, Enquirer, Oct. 8, 1824, 3; Whig, Oct. 8, 1824, 3
Smith, Thomas, Richmond, Whig, Dec. 29, 1835, 3
Smith, Thomas C., Richmond, Whig, Oct. 3, 1834, 1
Smith, Thomas G., King and Queen, Enquirer, April 18, 1823, 3
Smith, Thomas Perrin, [formerly of Princess Anne], Whig, May 22, 1832, 3
Smith, Virginia Cary, Richmond, Whig, March 23, 1832, 4
Smith, Capt. Wm., Louisa, Whig, Nov. 8, 1833, 3
Smith, William P., Richmond, Whig, Sept. 12, 1827, 3
Smither, Col. Gabriel, Culpeper, Enquirer, March 22, 1815, 3
Smoot, Amanda Ann, Culpeper, Whig, April 11, 1837, 3
Smoot, John James, Richmond, Whig, July 28, 1837, 2

Smyth, Mrs. Hannah, Richmond, Whig, Dec. 2, 1831, 3
Snead, Henry R., Albemarle, Enquirer, Dec. 31, 1811, 3
Snead, Samuel, Lunenburg, Enquirer, Oct. 3, 1828, 3
Snidow, Col. Christian, Giles, Whig, Oct. 14, 1836, 4
Smoot, Amanda Ann, Culpeper, Whig, April 11, 1837, 2
Snowden, Mrs. Cecilia, Richmond, Whig, Aug. 26, 1825, 3
Snowden, Capt. David, Richmond, Whig, Aug. 26, 1825, 3
Snowden, Joseph, Manchester, Enquirer, Oct. 12, 1821, 3
Snydor, Capt. William, Nottoway, Enquirer, Aug. 13, 1819, 3
Sockvider, Mrs. Mary, Richmond, Enquirer, Aug. 17, 1810, 3
Southall, Ann Bolling, Charles City, Enquirer, Oct. 27, 1820, 3
Southall, Eliza, Augusta, Nansemond, Whig, Aug. 1, 1831, 2
Southall, George, Cumberland, Whig, May 19, 1835, 1
Southall, Dr. Henry, Surry, Enquirer, March 30, 1827, 3
Southall, John, Richmond, Whig, July 14, 1835, 2
Southall, Mrs. Mary, Richmond, Whig, April 15, 1836, 3
Southall, Mrs. Mary, Charlottesville, Enquirer, Jan. 6, 1824, 3
Southall, Mary Ann, Amelia, Enquirer, March 2, 1822, 3
Southall, Philip V., Isle of Wight, Whig, June 28, 1836, 3
Southall, William W., Warminster, Enquirer, Dec. 11, 14, 1821, 3
Southgate, John, King and Queen, Enquirer, May 2, 1809, 3
Spark, Dr. Philip W., Mathews, Whig, Dec. 28, 1824, 3; Enquirer, Jan.
    15, 1825, 3
Speece, Dr. Charles, Halifax, Enquirer, Feb. 23, 1828, 3
Speece, Rev. Conrad, Richmond, Whig, Feb. 23, 1836, 1
Speed, John H., Mecklenburg, Enquirer, Sept. 11, 1818, 3
Spence, Dr. John, Dumfries, Whig, May 29, 1829, 3
Spence, Mrs. Sarah J., Henrico, Whig, Nov. 8, 1837, 2
Spencer, Thomas I., Charlotte, Enquirer, Jan. 21, 1823, 3
Spiller, Benjamin C., King William, Enquirer, Nov. 13, 1827, 3
Spiller, Mary, King William, Enquirer, July 11, 1826, 3
Spitler, Mrs. Bathsheba, Shenandoah, Enquirer, July 19, 1825, 3
Spooner, Mrs. Elizabeth, Petersburg, Whig, Dec. 23, 1830, 3
Spooner, Emily Sophia, Petersburg, Whig, Aug. 27, 1833, 1
Spottswood, Gen. Alexander, Spottsylvania, Enquirer, Dec. 31, 1818, 3
Spottswood, G. W., Orange, Whig, April 3, 1832, 1
Spracher, John Christopher, Wythe, Whig, June 9, 1830, 2
Stabler, Edward, Alexandria, Whig, Jan. 25, 1831, 3
Stalker, Mrs. Isabella, Richmond, Whig, Oct. 9, 1832, 1
Stanard, Beveley, Albemarle, Enquirer, Nov. 19, 1805, 3
Stanard, Edward Carter, Richmond, Enquirer, Dec. 15, 1810, 3
Stanard, Col. John, Richmond, Whig, Sept. 27, 1833, 2
Stanard, Mrs. Louisa, Richmond, Whig, April 30, 1824, 3
Stanard, Mrs. Mary, Orange, Whig, Feb. 16, 1831, 3
Stanard, Mary B., Chesterfield, Enquirer, Jan. 30, 1812, 3
Stanard, Mary Lucinda, Goochland, Whig, Feb. 22, 1825, 3
Stanard, Mrs. Robert, Richmond, Enquirer, April 30, 1824, 3
Stanton, Mrs. Grissella, ————————, Enquirer, July 21, 1818, 3
Staples, Mrs. Elizabeth D., Amherst, Whig, May 16, 1837, 4

Staples, John Edward, Patrick, Whig, Oct. 10, 1837, 2
Stark, Dr. Philip W., Mathews, Whig, Jan. 18, 1825, 3
Starke, Richard Fayett, Richmond, Whig, Sept. 30, 1834, 3
Starling, Jane G., King William, Enquirer, Dec. 21, 1824, 3; Whig, Dec. 28, 1824, 3
Starling, Capt. Roderick, King William, Enquirer, March 18, 1828, 3
Starr, Robert, Petersburg, Enquirer, Oct. 5, 1821, 3
Stearn, Frances, Prince Edward, Whig, April 26, 1834, 3
Steenbergen, Wm., Shenandoah, Whig, Jan. 7, 1835, 1
Steger, Elizabeth, Buckingham, Enquirer, Aug. 8, 1820, 3
Steger, Hardin Burnley, Hanover, Enquirer, Oct. 11, 1825, 3
Steger, Mrs. Judith Burnley, Powhatan, Enquirer, Feb. 14, 1826, 3
Steger, Mrs. Susan G., Powhatan, Enquirer, June 1, 1819, 3
Stephenson, Mrs. Augusta Virginia, Harper's Ferry, Whig, July 14, 1837, 2
Steptoe, James, New London, Enquirer, Feb. 25, 1826, 3
Stevens, Gen. Edward, Culpeper, Enquirer, Sept. 1, 1820, 3
Stevens, Mrs. Gilly, Culpeper, Enquirer, Jan. 2, 1821, 3
Stevens, Newton, Goochland, Enquirer, June 7, 1822, 3
Stevenson, Mrs. Andrew, Richmond, Enquirer, May 8, 1812, 3
Stewart, Mrs. Anna Maria, Campbell, Enquirer, May 28, 1819, 3
Stewart, Frederick Campbell, Westmoreland, Enquirer, July 24, 1827, 3
Stewart, Littleton W., Richmond, Whig, Sept. 26, 1837, 4
Stewart, William, Alexandria, Enquirer, Feb. 26, 1818, 3
Stith, Col. John, Brunswick, Enquirer, March 2, 1810, 3
Stith, James Brown, Richmond, Whig, May 21, 1833, 2
Stone, Juliet Elton, King and Queen, Whig, Aug. 11, 1837, 2
Stone, William S., Richmond, Whig, June 1, 1827, 3; Enquirer, June 1, 1827, 3
Storke, Catherine, King George, Enquirer, Aug. 2, 1805, 3
Storrow, Col. Samuel A., Culpeper, Whig, Jan. 27, 1837, 4
Stott, John, Henrico, Enquirer, Oct. 16, 1816, 3
Stout, Mrs. Maria Van Arsdalen, New Brunswick, Enquirer, Feb. 17, 1824, 4
Strachan, Mrs. Eliza H., Prince George, Whig, Aug. 16, 1825, 3
Strachan, John Blackwood, Petersburg, Whig, Nov. 4, 1830, 3
Strachan, Thomas, Spottsylvania, Enquirer, May 25, 1819, 3
Strange, Gideon A., Richmond, Whig, Feb. 27, 1838, 4
Strange, James, Petersburg, Enquirer, May 19, 1809, 3
Stras, George F., ————, Enquirer, Jan. 22, 1811, 3
Stratton, Edward, Northampton, Enquirer, June 15, 1827, 3
Stratton, John B., Bedford, Whig, June 26, 1830, 3
Stratton, Mrs. Polly, Powhatan, Enquirer, Jan. 5, 1821, 3
Straughan, Rev. Sam'l L., ————, Enquirer, June 19, 1821, 3
Street, Alfred, Richmond, Whig, Sept. 17, 1833, 4
Street, Mrs. Ann, Middlesex, Enquirer, Dec. 22, 1827, 3
Street, Madison, Richmond, Whig, Jan. 16, 1838, 1
Street, Mary Jane Williams, Richmond, Whig, March 8, 1838, 4
Street, Mrs. Patsy Perkins, Hanover, Enquirer, May 19, 1809, 3
Streshly, Thomas, Caroline, Enquirer, April 26, 1825, 3
Strickland, John, Botetourt, Whig, Nov. 21, 1834, 1

Strobia, John, Richmond, Enquirer, March 17, 1809, 3
Strong, Gov. ————————, Northampton, Enquirer, Nov. 19, 1819, 3
Stroria [Strobia], Francis, Richmond, Enquirer, March 1, 1815, 3
Stuart, Archibald, Richmond, Whig, July 17, 1832, 3
Stubblefield, Evey, Charles City, Whig, Feb. 23, 1838, 2
Stubbs, Capt. John Smith, King and Queen, Enquirer, May 6, 1823, 3
Stubbs, Lawrence, Gloucester, Enquirer, June 24, 1828, 3
Stubbs, Mrs. Martha Maria, Gloucester, Enquirer, Feb. 27, 1827, 3
Sublett, Harriet, Richmond, Enquirer, June 15, 1827, 3
Summers, George, Kanawha, Enquirer, Jan. 31, 1818, 3
Swann, John S., Rocky Mills, Enquirer, Sept. 12, 1817, 3
Swann, Mrs. Nancy, Manchester, Whig, May 25, 1832, 1
Swann, Samuel, Powhatan, Whig, June 9, 1830, 2
Swanson, Mrs. Elizabeth, Pittsylvania, Whig, Aug. 2, 1836, 1
Swearingen, Col. Joseph, Shepherdstown, Enquirer, Aug. 24, 1821, 3
Swinton, Mrs. Anna, Caroline, Enquirer, Sept. 1, 1820, 3
Swoope, Wm. M., Richmond, Whig, Sept. 4, 1830, 3
Sydnor, Mrs. Ann, Petersburg, Whig, May 9, 1837, 2
Sydnor, Elizabeth G., Hanover, Enquirer, March 23, 1821, 3
Sydnor, Fortunatus, West Wood, Enquirer, July 26, 1811, 3
Sydnor, Joseph Royall, Lynchburg, Whig, Oct. 20, 1837, 1
Sydnor, Mrs. Margaret, Richmond, Whig, Sept. 13, 1833, 3
Sydnor, Capt. William, Nottoway, Enquirer, Aug. 13, 1819, 3
Syme, Mrs. Elizabeth, Hanover, Enquirer, Aug. 7, 1807, 2
Syme, Mrs. Francis, Henrico, Whig, Feb. 27, 1828, 3; Enquirer, Feb. 23, 1828, 3
Syme, John M., Richmond, Whig, July 29, 1836, 3
Syme, Mary Elizabeth, Richmond, Whig, April 6, 1832, 1
Syme, Mrs. Sarah, Rocky Mills, Enquirer, Nov. 23, 1810, 3

T.

Tabb, Mrs. Frances, Amelia, Whig, April 26, 1828, 3; Enquirer, April 25, 1828, 3
Tabb, Mrs. Hester, Mathews, Enquirer, Feb. 13, 1823, 3
Tabb, Mrs. Lucy, Gloucester, Enquirer, Nov. 30, 1821, 3
Tabb, Philip, Gloucester, Enquirer, April 9, 1822, 3
Tabb, Thomas, Powhatan, Enquirer, Jan. 10, 1818, 3
Tabb, Thomas T. T., Gloucester, Whig, June 30, 1835, 4
Talbot, George A., Richmond, Whig, Oct. 13, 1829, 3
Taliaferro, Eliza, Caroline, Whig, Jan. 9, 1838, 4
Taliaferro, George Lawrence, ————————, Enquirer, Feb. 23, 1826, 3
Taliaferro, John H. Fitzhugh, Rose Hill, Enquirer, Nov. 21, 1826, 3
Taliaferro, Mrs. Lucy, Orange, Enquirer, May 19, 1826, 3
Taliaferro, Mrs. Lucy T., King George, Whig, Sept. 11, 1832, 2
Taliaferro, Mrs. Martha, Lynchburg, Enquirer, March 28, 1820, 3
Taliaferro, Merriwether, King George, Whig, Dec. 28, 1824, 3
Taliaferro, Robert H., ————————, Enquirer, July 1, 1807, 3
Taliaferro, Wm. F., Westmoreland, Whig, June 3, 1836, 2

Taliaferro, William Hickman, King William, Enquirer, Aug. 20, 1822, 3
Taliaferro, Mrs. William R. [Mary W.], Westmoreland, Whig, April 4, 1837, 1
Talley, James, Sr., Chesterfield, Whig, Oct. 28, 1829, 3
Tankersley, Col. Reuben, Caroline, Enquirer, Sept. 30, 1823, 3
Tapp, Walter H., Richmond, Whig, March 20, 1838, 2
Tapscott, Baker, Jefferson, Whig, May 8, 1838, 1
Tapscott, Mrs. Louisa W., Amherst, Whig, Dec. 8, 1827, 3
Tapscott, Wilson Nicholas, Buckingham, Enquirer, April 17, 1827, 3
Tarbill, Mrs. Eliza, Gosport, Enquirer, Oct. 9, 1821, 3
Tardy, Wm. O. P., Lynchburg, Whig, March 13, 1838, 3
Tate, Mrs. Ann, Richmond, Whig, Dec. 11, 1832, 1
Tate, Joseph, Richmond, Whig, Jan. 21, 1832, 1
Tate, Robert, Augusta, Whig, July 17, 1832, 3
Tatum, Ella Claiborne, Chesterfield, Whig, Oct. 27, 1831, 4
Tayloe, George Plator Forrest, Richmond, Enquirer, June 5, 1821, 3
Tayloe, John, Mount Airy, Whig, March 5, 1828, 3; Enquirer, March 7, 1828, 3
Tayloe, John, Richmond, Enquirer, May 18, 1824, 3
Tayloe, Lundsford, Bellona Arsenal, Whig, July 25, 1827, 3; Enquirer, July 27, 1827, 3
Taylor, Judge Allen, Richmond, Whig, June 14, 1836, 3
Taylor, Mrs. Ann, Orange, Enquirer, Jan. 6, 1824, 4
Taylor, Ann Elizabeth, Richmond, Whig, Feb. 1, 1832, 3
Taylor, Archibald, Richmond, Whig, Sept. 25, 1832, 3
Taylor, Beverley C., Richmond, Enquirer, May 3, 1808, 3
Taylor, Creed, Cumberland, Whig, Jan. 26, 1836, 1
Taylor, Daniel T., Richmond, Whig, Aug. 23, 1836, 2
Taylor, Col. Edmund, Cabell, Enquirer, Oct. 7, 10, 1823, 3
Taylor, Edmund, Hanover, Enquirer, Feb. 5, 1822, 3
Taylor, Mrs. Elizabeth Woodson, Nottoway, Enquirer, Aug. 22, 1828, 3
Taylor, Mrs. Frances, Orange, Whig, Oct. 27, 1831, 4
Taylor, George Keith, Petersburg, Enquirer, Nov. 11, 1815, 3
Taylor, George K., Accomac, Whig, Oct. 25, 1836, 2
Taylor, James, Richmond, Whig, Aug. 20, 1833, 2
Taylor, Col. John, Caroline, Whig, Aug. 27, 1824, 3; Enquirer, Aug. 27, 1824, 3 [2 places]
Taylor, Col. John, Caroline, Enquirer, March 18, 1828, 3
Taylor, Mrs. Martha, Lunenburg, Enquirer, March 21, 1828, 3
Taylor, Mary Ann, Richmond, Whig, Oct. 13, 1830, 3
Taylor, Mrs. Narcissa, Powhatan, Enquirer, July 27, 1821, 3
Taylor, Nathaniel C., Richmond, Enquirer, Nov. 27, 1807, 3
Taylor, Mrs. Obedience, Halifax, Enquirer, Oct. 28, 1815, 3
Taylor, Rebecca, Richmond, Enquirer, July 29, 1828, 3
Taylor, Richardson, [formerly of Richmond], Whig, Jan. 28, 1836, 1
Taylor, Robert, Norfolk, Enquirer, Oct. 17, 1826, 3
Taylor, Robert, Powhatan, Whig, July 21, 1826, 3; Enquirer, July 18, 1826, 3; Sept. 8, 1826, 3
Taylor, Robert, Richmond, Enquirer, Oct. 17, 1826, 3

Taylor, Judge Robert B., Norfolk, Whig, April 17, 1834, 1
Taylor, Mrs. Sarah, Hanover, Enquirer, Dec. 9, 1815, 3
Taylor, Thomas, Richmond, Whig, March 23, 1832, 3
Taylor, Dr. Thomas A., Powhatan, Whig, Dec. 5, 1828, 3
Taylor, Thomas Osborne, Chesterfield, Whig, Jan. 28, 1835, 1
Taylor, Timothy T., New Kent, Whig, Aug. 23, 1833, 1
Taylor, Gen. Waller, Lunenburg, Enquirer, Sept. 8, 1826, 3
Taylor, Capt. William, ————, Enquirer, Oct. 13, 1809, 3
Taylor, William, Lunenburg, Enquirer, Sept. 22, 1820, 3
Taylor, William F., Orange, Enquirer, Feb. 4, 1823, 3
Taylor, Wm. H., Richmond, Whig, Jan. 27, 1826, 3
Taylor, William Roscow, New Kent, Enquirer, March 17, 1818, 3
Tazewell, Mrs. Catharine, Boydton, Enquirer, Dec. 20, 1823, 3; Jan. 6, 1824, 3
Tazewell, Jane Rebecca Roberson, Chesterfield, Whig, Oct. 6, 1831, 4
Teagle, Edwin A., Williamsburg, Whig, May 5, 1838, 4
Tebbs, Mrs. Sarah, Essex, Enquirer, March 7, 1826, 3
Temple, Mrs., King William, Enquirer, May 10, 1822, 3
Temple, Mrs. Jack, King William, Enquirer, May 10, 1822, 3
Temple, Mrs. Lucy, King and Queen, Enquirer, Oct. 5, 1824, 3
Temple, Mrs. Maria D., Hanover Court House, Whig, Feb. 28, 1837, 4
Temple, Mrs. Molly, King William, Enquirer, Aug. 18, 1820, 3
Temple, Robert, Chesterfield, Whig, Dec. 29, 1835, 2
Terril, Mrs. Emily Ann, Eastern Shore, Whig, Sept. 28, 1832, 1
Terrill, Maria, Richmond, Enquirer, Sept. 16, 1823, 3
Terry, Mrs. Agnes, Huntsville, Enquirer, Dec. 30, 1825, 3
Terry, Obadiah P., Pittsylvania, Whig, April 18, 1837, 4
Terry, S. Q., ————, Enquirer, May 12, 1809, 3
Terry, Col. William, Halifax, Enquirer, Dec. 25, 1810, 3
Thilman, John D., Hanover, Enquirer, Dec. 20, 1823, 3
Thilman, Mrs. Mary, Hanover, Whig, Nov. 15, 1833, 1
Thoasson [Thomasson], Overton, Louisa, Whig, May 16, 1834, 4
Tholson, Hon. Thomas, Brunswick, Enquirer, July 13, 1816, 3
Thomas, Urbanna, ————, Enquirer, Aug. 27, 1813, 2
Thomas, Claiborne L., Richmond, Whig, Nov. 8, 1833, 1
Thomas, Daniel M. H., Richmond, Whig, Sept. 24, 1833, 2
Thomas, Elizabeth, Caroline, Enquirer, Jan. 6, 1824, 4
Thomas, Elizabeth, Cumberland, Enquirer, Nov. 19, 1824, 3
Thompson, Belfour, Richmond, Enquirer, Sept. 11, 1812, 3
Thompson, Charles, Sr., Hanover, Whig, March 29, 1836, 1
Thompson, Capt. Garland, Hanover, Enquirer, May 8, 1821, 3
Thompson, Garland, Richmond, Whig, May 15, 1835, 4
Thompson, James, Tazewell, Enquirer, Aug. 21, 1821, 3
Thompson, John, Nelson, Whig, Aug. 9, 22, 1828, 3
Thompson, Matthew, Augusta, Enquirer, April 19, 1822, 3
Thompson, Richard, Richmond, Enquirer, Jan. 6, 1810, 3
Thompson, William, Bedford, Enquirer, April 29, 1823, 1
Thomson, Nathaniel, Hanover, Enquirer, Aug. 16, 1805, 3
Thornton, Mrs. Eliza, near Caira, Enquirer, Sept. 26, 1828, 3

Index to Obituary Notices

77

Thornton, Elizabeth T., Cumberland, Enquirer, Sept. 19, 1823, 3
Thornton, George Washington, Orange, Enquirer, Dec. 19, 1816, 3
Thornton, John, Hanover, Enquirer, Jan. 29, 1822, 3
Thornton, John S., Richmond, Whig, Oct. 17, 1837, 4
Thornton, John T., Cumberland, Enquirer, Aug. 19, 1823, 3
Thornton, Mrs. Lavinnia, Buckingham, Whig, July 31, 1838, 4
Thornton, Mary I. B., and Elizabeth T., children of Capt. W. M. Thornton, Cumberland, Enquirer, Sept. 19, 1823, 3
Thornton, Peter, Caroline, Whig, Oct. 11, 1833, 1
Thornton, Thomas C., Hanover, Whig, Oct. 17, 1837, 4
Thornton, Thomas Griffin, Richmond, Whig, Nov. 2, 1830, 3
Thruston, James, Rockingham, Whig, May 19, 1829, 3
Thweatt, Maj. Giles, Halifax, Enquirer, Nov. 21, 1823, 3
Tibbs [Tebbs ?], Mrs. Nancy, Essex, Enquirer, May 7, 1822, 3
Timberlake, Mrs. Emily R., Richmond, Whig, Nov. 22, 1836, 3
Timberlake, Mrs. Elizabeth R., King William, Whig, July 15, 1836, 1
Timberlake, Francis, Hanover, Enquirer, March 15, 1808, 3
Timberlake, Joseph, Norfolk, Enquirer, Sept. 4, 1821, 3
Timberlake, Matthew, Hanover, Enquirer, Feb. 11, 1808, 3
Timberlake, Mrs. Mildred, Hanover, Enquirer, Jan. 30, 1810, 3
Timberlake, Sarah, Hanover, Whig, Jan. 26, 1832, 3
Timberlake, Mrs. Welhelmina Jones, Fluvanna, Enquirer, March 25, 1825, 3
Tinsley, Mrs. Ann, Goochland, Whig, July 22, 1836, 2
Tinsley, Capt. Parke, Hanover, Enquirer, Jan. 6, 13, 1825, 3
Tinsley, Peter, Richmond, Enquirer, July 24, 1810, 3
Tinsley, Capt. Samuel, Hanover, Whig, Nov. 1, 1833, 3
Tinsley, Mrs. Sarah Ann, Danville, Whig, Dec. 16, 1836, 2
Tinsley, Col. Thomas, Hanover, Enquirer, Jan. 2, 1823, 3
Tisdale, William, Petersburg, Enquirer, Nov. 27, 1818, 3
Tod, Mrs. Elizabeth M., Caroline, Enquirer, Dec. 12, 1826, 3
Todd, Mrs. Frances, King and Queen, Enquirer, June 20, 1820, 3
Todd, Miles, Richmond, Enquirer, Nov. 25, 1817, 3
Toler, Mrs. Cynthia, Richmond, Whig, Nov. 14, 1829, 3
Toler, Mrs. Mary, Caroline, Enquirer, Nov. 26, 1813, 3
Toler, Mrs. Mary Ann Frances, Richmond, Whig, Oct. 30, 1835, 1
Toler, William, Hanover, Whig, Dec. 25, 1830, 3
Tomkies, William, Gloucester, Enquirer, March 2, 1824, 3
Tomlin, John W., Hanover, Enquirer, Dec. 7, 1815, 3
Tomkins, Catharine, King William, Whig, Jan. 6, 1832, 1
Tompkins, Maj. Christopher, Richmond, Enquirer, Jan. 10, 1826, 3
Tompkins, Christopher, Matthews, Whig, Aug. 28, 1838, 4
Tompkins, Christopher, Richmond, Whig, Jan. 10, 1826, 3
Tompkins, Henry, Richmond, Whig, April 18, 1829, 3
Tompkins, Rev. James, Lynchburg, Enquirer, Aug. 1, 1806, 3
Tompkins, James O., Richmond, Enquirer, April 23, 1824, 3
Tompkins, Mrs. Martha, Richmond, Whig, May 17, 1834, 1
Toney, John, Powhatan, Whig, April 7, 1835, 4
Towler, Mrs. Sally, ————, Enquirer, March 16, 1819, 3
Towles, Col. Oliver, ————, Enquirer, Dec. 18, 1821, 3

Towles, Capt. Therit, Spottsylvania, Whig, Oct. 25, 1836, 1
Townes, Eliza M., Amelia, Whig, May 18, 1838, 4
Townes, Capt. Joseph, Mecklenburg, Enquirer, June 25, 1824, 3
Townsend, Gideon, Rocketts, Whig, May 12, 1837, 2
Trabue, Alexander Pendleton, Chesterfield, Whig, Jan. 20, 1837,
Trabue, Daniel, Chesterfield, Enquirer, Feb. 13, 1819, 3
Trabue, Mrs. Frances, Chesterfield, Whig, April 13, 1832, 4
Trabue, John, Chesterfield, Enquirer, April 18, 1828, 3; Whig, April 12,
    1828, 3
Trabue, Mrs. Priscella, Chesterfield, Enquirer, July 16, 1822, 3
Trabue, Capt. Wm., Chesterfield, Enquirer, May 4, 1827, 3
Travis, Col. Champion, Williamsburg, Enquirer, Sept. 4, 1810, 3
Travis, Samuel, Williamsburg, Enquirer, July 17, 20, 30, 1821, 3
Tredway, Mrs. Jane, Manchester, Enquirer, Oct. 31, 1806, 3
Trent, John A., Cumberland, Whig, July 31, 1838, 4
Trent, Mrs. Nancy, Richmond, Enquirer, April 11, 1828, 3; Whig, April
    12, 1828, 3
Trevilian, Thomas, Caroline, Whig, Dec. 2, 1825, 3; Enquirer, Dec. 2, 1825, 3
Trial, Stephen L., Fluvanna, Whig, Nov. 29, 1831, 3
Trice, Mrs. Catharine, ————, Enquirer, July 1, 1825, 3
Trigg, Hon. John, Bedford, Enquirer, July 28, 1804, 3
Triplett, Maj. Philip, Loudoun, Whig, July 6, 1832, 3
Trotter, Gen. Matthew, Richmond, Whig, Dec. 16, 1830, 3
Trower, John, Richmond, Enquirer, Aug. 31, 1816, 3
Trueheart, Barthomew, Powhatan, Whig, Dec. 15, 1834, 3
Trueheart, David Porter, Hanover, Whig, Oct. 8, 1829, 3
Trueheart, Mrs. Elizabeth, Hanover, Enquirer, Feb. 2, 1819, 3
Trueheart, Mrs. Maria D., Richmond, Enquirer, Aug. 19, 1817, 3
Tucker, Francis B., Winchester, Enquirer, Jan. 2, 1827, 3
Tucker, Dr. Henry Wm., Charlotte, Enquirer, Feb. 21, 1828, 3
Tucker, Henry St. George, Jr., Winchester, Whig, Feb. 28, 1826, 3
Tucker, Julianna, Brunswick, Whig, Aug. 16, 1825, 3
Tucker, Mrs. Lelia, Nelson, Whig, Oct. 3, 1837, 4
Tucker, Mrs. Maria, Lynchburg, Enquirer, Feb. 11, 1823, 3
Tucker, Mary S., Richmond, Enquirer, May 1, 1827, 3
Tucker, Hon. St. George, Warminster, Enquirer, Nov. 23, 1827, 3
Tunsdall, Lucy Caroline, Pittsylvania, Enquirer, June 30, 1826, 3
Tunstall, Robert P., King and Queen, Enquirer, Nov. 23, 1827, 3
Tunstill, Mrs. Amanda L., Richmond, Whig, July 21, 1837, 1
Tunstill, Mrs. Sarah, Amelia, Enquirer, March 28, 1828, 3
Turner, Mrs. Anne, Staunton, Enquirer, April 24, 1810, 3
Turner, Benjamin, Northumberland, Enquirer, Feb. 14, 1824, 3
Turner, Edmund Pendleton, Richmond, Enquirer, Oct. 22, 1822, 3
Turner, Henry, Powhatan, Enquirer, May 23, 1823, 3
Turner, James, King William, Whig, Feb. 11, 1825, 3
Turner, Mrs. Mary, Richmond, Whig, Dec. 13, 1825, 3; Enquirer, Dec. 17,
    1825, 3
Turner, Nancy, Richmond, Whig, March 29, 1831, 3
Turner, Mrs. Sally, Hanover, Enquirer, March 30, 1816, 3

Turner, Susan Baynton, Prince William, Whig, Aug. 3, 1830, 3
Turner, Wm., Caroline, Whig, Oct. 17, 1829, 2
Turpin, Mrs. Elizabeth, Henrico, Enquirer, Jan. 26, 1826, 3
Turpin, Emmeline G., Warwick, Whig, Aug. 21, 1832, 3; Aug. 24, 1832, 1
Turpin, Mrs. Harriet E., Henrico and Warwick, Whig, Dec. 13, 1825, 3
Turpin, Dr. Philip, Chesterfiefild, Whig, May 14, 1828, 3; Enquirer, May 17, 1828, 3
Turpin, Robertson, Chesterfield, Whig, Sept. 1, 1831, 2
Tyler, Emma Millicent, Richmond, Whig, Jan. 9, 1838, 2
Tyler, Capt. George, Spottsylvania, Whig, Feb. 5, 1833, 3
Tyler, Capt. Jabez, Rocketts, Whig, Feb. 23, 1833, 3
Tyler, Hon. John, —————, Enquirer, Jan. 12, 1813, 3
Tyler, John, Williamsburg, Enquirer, March 31, 1812, 3
Tyler, Lewis G., New Kent, Enquirer, May 7, 1822, 3
Tyler, Nathaniel, Fauquier, Whig, March 6, 1835, 1
Tyler, Thomas Waller, Hanover, Whig, Aug. 24, 1832, 1

U.

Underwood, Mrs. Jane, Hanover, Enquirer, April 27, 1821, 3
Underwood, John, Goochland, Whig, Oct. 6, 1837, 2
Underwood, Patsy, Richmond, Whig, Sept. 11, 1832, 2
Underwood, Thomas, Sr., Hanover, Enquirer, Feb. 1, 1815, 3
Upshaw, Edwin, Jr., King and Queen, Whig, March 8, 1838, 4
Upshaw, Col. James, Caroline, Enquirer, July 22, 1806, 3
Upshaw, Mrs. Martha Ann Elkton, —————, Enquirer, May 9, 1928, 3
Upshur, Caleb B., Northampton, Enquirer, March 3, 1821, 3
Upshur, Elizabeth W., Northampton, Enquirer, Dec. 11, 1817, 3
Upshur, John D., Northampton, Whig, Aug. 7, 1838, 2
Upshur, Littleton, Northampton, Enquirer, Sept. 6, 1811, 3
Upshur, Col. Lyttleton, Northampton, Whig, Oct. 19, 1832, 3; Whig, Oct. 26, 1832, 1
Upshur, Mary Evelina, Northampton, Whig, May 13, 1829, 3
Urquhart, Mrs. Maria A., Southampton, Whig, Nov. 6, 1835, 2
Urquhart, Mrs. Nancy, Southampton, Whig, Aug. 22, 1837, 2

V.

Vadin, Mrs. Sarah, Pittsylvania, Enquirer, Feb. 24, 1824, 3
Valentine, Benjamin B., Richmond, Whig, April 6, 1832, 1
VanBibber, Mrs. S. E., Mathews, Whig, April 19, 1836, 2
Vandewall, Col. Marks, Richmond, Enquirer, June 14, 1808, 3
VanDewson, George Baldwin, Richmond, Whig, Oct. 10, 1834, 4
Van Swearingen, Thomas, —————, Enquirer, Aug. 30, 1822, 3
Vaughan, Mrs. Elizabeth, Mecklenburg, Enquirer, Oct. 27, 1820, 3
Vaughan, Mrs. Mary, Goochland, Enquirer, Jan. 11, 1820, 3
Vaughan, Mary Jane, Goochland, Enquirer, Sept. 7, 1821, 3
Vaughan, Capt. Reuben, Mecklenburg, Enquirer, May 16, 1817, 3
Vauter, Benjamin, Richmond, Whig, May 3, 1830, 2

Venable, Col. Samuel W., ——————, Enquirer, Oct. 9, 1821, 3
Verser, Capt. Daniel, Nottoway, Enquirer, Dec. 14, 1826, 3
Vowles, George F., Stafford, Enquirer, Jan. 27, 1825, 3; Whig, Jan. 28, 1825, 3

W.

Waddell, Anderson M., Lynchburg, Whig, Oct. 5, 1832, 1
Waddell, Rev. James, Albemarle, Enquirer, Oct. 4, 1805, 3
Waddy, Benjamin, Louisa, Enquirer, June 8, 1827, 3
Waddy, John, Louisa, Enquirer, Oct. 22, 1819, 3
Wade, John B., Prince Edward, Enquirer, Sept. 10, 1822, 3
Wade, Samuel P., Louisa, Enquirer, Aug. 28, 1821, 3
Walford, Anne, ——————, Enquirer, May 29, 1812, 3
Walford, Mrs. Susanna, Richmond, Enquirer, March 18, 1806, 3
Walker, Dr., Petersburg, Enquirer, July 20, 1816, 3
Walker, Elizabeth Jane, Richmond, Whig, Sept. 19, 1829, 3
Walker, Georgianna, Richmond, Whig, July 4, 1837, 2
Walker, Mrs. Jane B., Albemarle, Enquirer, Feb. 26, 1808, 3
Walker, John, Albemarle, Enquirer, Jan. 2, 1810, 3
Walker, John, Buckingham, Enquirer, Aug. 22, 1828, 3
Walker, John, Henrico, Enquirer, March 7, 1826, 3
Walker, Dr. John U., Brunswick, Enquirer, May 9, 1827, 3
Walker, John Patrick, Buckingham, Enquirer, June 24, 1828, 3
Walker, Mrs. Maria, Richmond, Whig, Sept. 1, 1831, 1
Walker, Mrs. Mary, Buckingham, Enquirer, Oct. 5, 1821, 3
Walker, Mrs. Mary Jane, Buckingham, Whig, Oct. 2, 1830, 3
Walker, Mrs. Martha Ann, Richmond, Whig, Oct. 2, 1835, 2
Walker, Sarah M., Charles City, Whig, Feb. 13, 1838,
Walker, Mrs. Susan, Bedford, Enquirer, Oct. 30, 1827, 3
Walker, Thomas, Charles City, Enquirer, Feb. 6, 1808, 3
Walker, Thomas, Charles City, Whig, Jan. 16, 1835, 4
Waller, Mrs. Eliza C., Williamsburg, Enquirer, July 15, 1823, 3
Waller, Mrs. Elizabeth, Amherst, Enquirer, June 4, 1822, 3
Waller, James, Stafford, Enquirer, Feb. 10, 1824, 3
Waller, John Walker, York, Enquirer, May 29, 1813, 3
Waller, Mrs. Mary, Williamsburg, Enquirer, May 1, 1827, 3
Waller, Col. Wm., Williamsburg, Whig, Dec. 15, 1834, 1
Waller, Rev. William E., Spottsylvania, Whig, Aug. 4, 1830, 3
Waller, Withers, Stafford, Enquirer, Dec. 10, 1825, 3
Walthall, John Marshall, Richmond, Whig, Feb. 9, 1836, 3
Walthall, Mrs. Mary, Buckingham, Enquirer, Aug. 27, 1819, 2
Walthall, Mrs. Mary Ann L., Richmond, Whig, July 12, 1833, 3
Walton, Mrs. Mary, Pittsylvania, Whig, March 12, 1833, 1
Walton, Mrs. Nancy, Cumberland, Enquirer, March 29, 1825, 3
Ward, Henry, Lynchburg, Whig, March 13, 1835, 2
Ward, Jeremiah, Cabell, Enquirer, May 18, 1824, 3
Ward, Joel, Berkley, Whig, Jan. 27, 1837, 4
Ward, Robert, near Danville, Whig, June 12, 1835, 3

Ward, Sarah Ann, Dinwiddie, Whig, Dec. 12, 1828, 3
Warden, Hugh, —————, Enquirer, April 2, 1811, 3
Warden, John, Richmond, Enquirer, Feb. 12, 1814, 3
Wardlaw, Mrs. Sarah, Richmond, Enquirer, April 26, 1808, 3
Ware, Mrs. Hannah Clarke, New Kent, Enquirer, Dec. 3, 1805, 3
Ware, James, Goochland, Enquirer, July 14, 1818, 3
Ware, John, Dumfries, Enquirer, Aug. 23, 1805, 3
Waring, Epaphroditus Lawson, Westmoreland, Enquirer,, May 25, 1821, 3
Warrell, James, Richmond, Whig, Aug. 11, 1827, 3
Warren, Mrs. Jane, New Kent, Whig, Nov. 5, 1830, 3
Warren, John, New Kent, Enquirer, July 7, 1826, 3
Warren, Lilla, Richmond, Whig, Aug. 4, 1831, 3
Warren, Richard A., New Kent, Enquirer, June 10, 1825, 3
Warren, Robert, Manchester, Whig, Sept. 26, 1834, 1
Warren, Robert, King William, Enquirer, Oct. 15, 1822, 3
Warwick, Jacob, Pocahontas, Enquirer, Jan. 31, 1826, 3
Warwick, Mrs. Julia, Richmond, Whig, April 19, 1836, 1
Warwick, Mrs. Sally, Richmond, Enquirer, June 6, 1826, 3; Whig, June 6, 1826, 3
Warwick, Maj. Wm., Lynchburg, Whig, Aug. 24, 1832, 1
Washington, Mrs. Elizabeth B., Jefferson, Whig, Nov. 3, 1837, 1
Washington, Col. William, —————, Enquirer, April 6, 1810, 4
Washington, Wm. Augustine, Westmoreland, Whig, July 9, 16, 1830, 3
Washington, Col. William Augustine, Enquirer, Oct. 12, 1810, 3
Waterman, Asher, Harrisonburg, Enquirer, May 15, 1827, 3
Waters, Dr. Robert, Jefferson, Whig, Dec. 19, 1837, 2
Watkins, Augustus, Prince Edward, Enquirer, Oct. 11, 1825, 3; Whig, Oct. 14, 1825, 3
Watkins, Benjamin, Chesterfield, Enquirer, Aug. 13, 1825, 3; Whig, Aug. 16, 1825, 3
Watkins, Mrs. Catharine, Goochland, Whig, March 26, 1832, 3
Watkins, Claiborne, Powhatan, Whig, Dec. 19, 1829, 3 .
Watkins, Edward, Powhatan, Whig, April 14, 1835, 3
Watkins, Maj. H. W., Powhatan, Enquirer, Jan. 1, 1828, 3
Watkins, Maj. Henry Walthall, Powhatan, Enquirer, Dec. 20, 1827, 3
Watkins, Col. Joel, Buckingham, Enquirer, Aug. 3, 1824, 3
Watkins, Col. Joel, Charlotte, Enquirer, Jan. 11, 1820, 3
Watkins, Joel, Powhatan, Enquirer, Oct. 18, 1822, 3
Watkins, Mrs. John [Lucy Ann], Richmond, Whig, April 11, 1837, 4
Watkins, Col. John D., New Kent, Whig, April 30, 1833, 3; May 7, 1833, 2
Watkins, Louisa Nivison, Goochland, Enquirer, June 24, 1828, 3
Watkins, Dr. Mayo C., Goochland, Enquirer, June 8, 1813, 3
Watkins, Dr. Thomas, Albemarle, Enquirer, March 7, 1823, 3
Watkins, Thomas, Chesterfield, Enquirer, Jan. 11, 1812, 3
Watkins, Thomas, Sr., Halifax, Enquirer, Aug. 21, 1816, 3
Watkins, William, Hanover, Enquirer, Feb. 28, 1817, 3
Watson, Mrs. Ann Caroline, Richmond, Enquirer, May 28, 1822, 3
Watson, Lieut. Col. Augustus, Prince Edward, Enquirer, Feb. 1, 1815, 1
Watson, Mrs. Elizabeth, Boydton, Enquirer, July 20, 1827, 3

Watson, Joseph Shelton, Louisa, Enquirer, Oct. 8, 1805, 2
Watson, Matthew, Albemarle, Enquirer, Oct. 22, 1822, 3
Watson, Mrs. Polly, Buckingham, Enquirer, Nov. 16, 1824, 3
Watt, Lieut., ————, Enquirer, June 25, 1813, 3
Watt, Mrs. Betsey W., Buckingham, Enquirer, June 8, 1814, 3
Watt, Margaret M., Richmond, Whig, Dec. 30, 1831, 1
Watts, Mrs. Eliza Horsley, Albemarle, Whig, Aug. 15, 1837, 2
Watts, Col. John, Bedford, Whig, June 14, 1830, 3
Watts, Thomas J., Petersburg, Whig, July 8, 1834, 3
Wauhop, Victor, Richmond, Enquirer, Oct. 12, 1819, 3
Weaver, Mrs. Mary, Columbia, Enquirer, Aug. 3, 1821, 3
Weaver, Mrs. Matilda, Goochland, Enquirer, Nov. 2, 1824, 3
Webb, Mrs. Catharine, Hanover, Enquirer, Sept. 17, 1811, 3
Webb, Mrs. Elizabeth G., Williamsburg, Whig, June 23, 1826, 3; Enquirer,
     June 27, 1826, 3
Webb, James, King and Queen, Whig, Feb. 28, 1832, 3
Webb, Maj. John S., New Kent, Enquirer, Nov. 3, 1822, 3
Webb, Col. Richard D., Suffolk, Whig, July 27, 1836, 2
Webster, Mrs. Ann S., Richmond, Whig, Jan. 28, 1825, 3
Webster, Isaac, Chesterfield, Enquirer, March 9, 1816, 3
Weems, Rev. Mason L., Dumfries, Enquirer, July 1, 1825, 3
Weisiger, Mrs. Elizabeth, Richmond, Whig, July 29, 1834, 1
Welch, Arthur S., ————, Enquirer, Oct. 5, 1827, 3
Welch, David T., Richmond, Whig, Sept. 6, 1825, 3
Welch, Mrs. Mary, Chesterfield, Enquirer, Nov. 2, 1821, 3
Welch, Capt. P. T., Chesterfield, Enquirer, Sept. 2, 1825, 3
Welford, Dr. Horner, Richmond, Enquirer, June 3, 1828, 3
Weller, Withers, Stafford, Enquirer, Aug. 10, 1827, 3
Wellford, Mrs. Betty Burwell, Fredericksburg, Enquirer, Sept. 3, 1819, 3
Wellford, Dr. Robert, Fredericksburg, Enquirer, April 29, 1823, 3; May
     2, 1823, 3
Wells, James E., Richmond, Whig, June 6, 1837, 2
Wells, Thomas, Charlottesville, Enquirer, Aug. 27, 1822, 3
Wercq, Victoire, Richmond, Whig, Dec. 28, 1829, 2
Werg, Lewis, ————, Enquirer, Dec. 15, 1812, 3
West, Mrs., Jr., ————, Enquirer, Jan. 22, 1805, 3
West, Mrs. Polly, Richmond, Whig, March 15, 1830, 3
West, Wm. W., Northampton, Whig, Oct. 25, 1836, 1
Westmore, Mrs. Eliza, Dunkirk, Enquirer, Sept. 17, 1819, 3
Westwood, William J., Hampton, Whig, Sept. 15, 1827, 3
Weymouth, Mrs. Mary S., Richmond, Whig, Nov. 18, 1834, 1
Wheaton, Mrs. Sarah, Richmond, Whig, Aug. 25, 1826, 3
Wheeler, ————, Chesterfield, Whig, July 19, 1830, 3
Wheeler, Luke, Norfolk, Enquirer, Aug. 17, 1827, 3
Wheeley, Prufanda, King William, Whig, Aug. 3, 1838, 1
Whitaker, Anthony, Richmond, Enquirer, March 18, 1828, 3; Whig, March
     12, 22, 1828, 3
Whitaker, Sarah S., Richmond, Whig, April 27, 1832, 3
Whitaker, William, Richmond, Enquirer, Oct. 21, 1806, 3

White, Alexander, —————, Enquirer, Oct. 17, 1804, 3
White, Mrs. Elizabeth, Hanover, Enquirer, Dec. 21, 1815, 3
White, Harriman, Richmond, Whig, Feb. 28, 1826, 3
White, Mrs. Judith, King William, Enquirer, Oct. 21, 1823, 3
White, Mrs. Margaret Ann, Richmond, Whig, Dec. 12, 1837, 2
White, Mrs. Martha G., Richmond, Enquirer, March 7, 1826, 3
White, Mrs. Mary Ann, Caroline, Enquirer, Jan. 24, 1822, 3
White, Hon. Robert, Winchester, Whig, March 16, 1831, 3
White, Mrs. Sarah W., Richmond, Whig, Dec. 15, 1835, 3
White, Thomas, Hanover, Whig, March 29, 1825, 3
White, Gen. Thomas, Hanover, Enquirer, April 12, 1825, 3
White, Thomas H., Richmond, Whig, Oct. 9, 1832, 3
White, Col. William, Orange, Enquirer, Sept. 2, 1828, 3
White, Capt, William, Hanover, Enquirer, Sept. 15, 1820, 3
White, Wm., Charlotte, Enquirer, Jan. 3, 1828, 3
White, William M., James City, Enquirer, Oct. 17, 1823, 3
Whitehead, Benjamin, Buckingham, Whig, Aug. 3, 1838, 2
Whiting, Agatha Randolph, Middlesex, Enquirer, Jan. 21, 1823, 3
Whiting, Francis, Gloucester, Enquirer, Jan. 31, 1826, 3
Whiting, Mrs. Hannah, Frederick, Enquirer, Aug. 14, 1827, 3
Whiting, Mrs. Harriet, Jefferson, Enquirer, Sept. 12, 1826, 3
Whiting, Lewis Skaife, Richmond, Whig, July 28, 1835, 2
Whiting, Mary B., Frederick, Enquirer, Nov. 20, 1827, 3
Whiting, Mrs. Mary Hartwell, Gloucester, Enquirer, Dec. 30, 1823, 3
Whiting, Susan B., Gloucester, Enquirer, May 18, 1816, 4
Whitlock, Mrs. Charles, Richmond, Enquirer, April 2, 1811, 3
Whitlock, John, Chesterfield, Whig, Sept. 23, 1825, 3
Whitlock, Mrs. Martha B., Richmond, Enquirer, March 20, 1818, 3
Whitlock, Sarah, Hanover, Enquirer, June 19, 1821, 3
Whitlocke, Charles, Richmond, Enquirer, Aug. 25, 1820, 3
Whitlocke, Izard Bacon, Richmond, Whig, May 31, 1825, 3
Whitworth, Elizabeth Jane, Buckingham, Enquirer, July 11, 1828, 3
Wiatt, James C., Gloucester, Enquirer, Oct. 14, 1824, 3
Wiatt, John, Lynchburg, Whig, March 2, 1827, 3
Wiatt, Peter, Gloucester, Whig, Oct. 8, 1824, 3; Enquirer, Oct. 14, 1824, 3
Wicker, Mrs. Nancy T., Hanover, Whig, July 19, 1836, 3
Wigglesworth, Maj. Claiborne, Fredericksburg, Enquirer, June 16, 1826, 3
Wight, Mrs. Augusta M., Richmond, Whig, June 16, 1830, 3
Wight, Hezekiah L., Goochland, Whig, July 14, 1837, 4
Wilkerson, Thomas L., Richmond, Enquirer, March 22, 1822, 3
Wilkinson, George B., —————, Whig, Nov. 22, 1825, 3
Wilkinson, Capt. James, New Kent, Enquirer, Feb. 25, 1822, [23], 3
Wilkinson, Capt. James B., —————, Enquirer, Oct. 29, 1813, 3
Willcox, Mrs. Jane W., Charles City, Whig, Dec. 4, 1832, 1
Willey, Mrs. Hannah, Richmond, Enquirer, March 15, 1822, 3
Williams, Mrs. Ann E. J., Richmond, Enquirer, Sept. 27, 1825, 3
Williams, Beverly Julius, New Kent, Whig, Aug. 14, 1838, 2
Williams, Mrs. Christian, Whig, June 3, 1836, 2
Williams, Gen. David R., Richmond, Whig, Nov. 25, 1830, 2

Williams, Mrs. E. J., Chesterfield, Enquirer, Sept. 27, 1825, 3
Williams, Elisha, Bath, Enquirer, Dec. 15, 1812, 3
Williams, George, Richmond, Whig, June 26, 1832, 3
Williams, George J., Harrison, Whig, May 2, 1834, 2
Williams, Mrs. Grizel Bowie, Fredericksburg, Enquirer, April 29, 1823, 3
Williams, James, Richmond, Whig, Jan. 24, 1832, 1
Williams, Jared, Winchester, Whig, Jan. 19, 1831, 3
Williams, Mrs. Margaret, Richmond, Whig, Nov. 16, 1832, 4
Williams, Mrs. Mary, Halifax, Enquirer, Dec. 3, 1819, 3
Williams, Montague, King William, Enquirer, Aug. 14, 1812, 3
Williams, Samuel, Petersburg, Enquirer, Oct. 1, 1813, 3
Williams, Tarleton, Cumberland, Enquirer, Sept. 9, 1823, 3
Williams, William C., Shenandoah, Enquirer, Oct. 21, 1817, 3
Williamson, Mrs. Ann, Richmond, Enquirer, May 8, 1827, 3
Williamson, Cary, Charles City, Whig, Dec. 4, 1832, 3
Williamson, Capt. George, Powhatan, Enquirer, April 9, 1824, 3
Williamson, Capt. George, Richmond, Whig, May 20, 1825, 3
Williamson, George, Richmond, Whig, Jan. 2, 1835, 1
Williamson, James, Bedford, Whig, July 16, 1833, 1
Williamson, John, Richmond, Enquirer, April 26, 1815, 3
Williamson, Mrs. Sarah, Richmond, Whig, Dec. 19, 1831, 4
Williamson, Susannah, Henrico, Whig, Jan. 26, 1838, 4
Willing, Thomas, Richmond, Enquirer, Jan. 23, 1821, 3
Willis, Benjamin, Louisa, Enquirer, Aug. 7, 1821, 3
Willis, Mrs. Eliza, Culpeper, Enquirer, April 16, 1824, 3
Wills, Edmund, Nottoway, Whig, April 21, 1826, 3
Wills, Elias, Fluvanna, Enquirer, Oct. 8, 1805, 2
Wills, George, James City, Whig, March 8, 1838, 4
Wills, Horatio, Fluvanna, Enquirer, May 4, 1827, 3
Wills, Dr. John, Fluvanna, Enquirer, Oct. 4, 1815, 3
Wilmer, Rev. Wm. H., D. D., Williamsburg, Enquirer, July 31, 1827, 3;
     Whig, July 28, 1827, 3
Wilson, Edward D., Portsmouth, Enquirer, Aug. 3, 1821, 3
Wilson, Mrs. Elizabeth, Richmond, Whig, May 17, 1836, 1
Wilson, Frederick T., ————, Whig, Nov. 10, 1830, 3
Wilson, George Maxwell, Albemarle, Whig, June 29, 1838, 1
Wilson, John, Norfolk, Enquirer, Aug. 28, 1821, 3
Wilson, Leonard, Halifax, Enquirer, Nov. 19, 1805, 3
Wilson, Mrs. Mary, Richmond, Whig, Sept. 30, 1834, 3
Wilson, Richard, Cumberland, Whig, Feb. 7, 1837, 3
Wilson, Richard, Cumberland, Enquirer, Feb. 8, 1827, 3
Wilson, Thomas, Richmond, Enquirer, May 5, 1818, 3
Wimbish, Maj. John, Halifax, Enquirer, Jan. 9, 1819, 4
Wimbish, Mrs. Nancy, Halifax, Whig, April 5, 1836, 3
Wimbish, Sarah C., Halifax, Enquirer, Jan. 23, 1816, 3
Winfree, Adelaide, Chesterfield, Whig, Oct. 6, 1831, 3
Winfree, Mrs. Lucy, Lynchburg, Whig, March 24, 1836, 3
Wingfield, Henry L., Cartersville, Enquirer, July 16, 1822, 3
Winn, John, Charlottesville, Whig, Nov. 21, 1837, 2

Winn, Wm. C., Richmond, Enquirer, May 8, 1827, 3
Winslow, Mrs. S. P., ————, Enquirer, Sept. 2, 1823, 4
Winston, Mrs. Ann K., Hanover, Enquirer, July 10, 1812, 3
Winston, Mrs. Dorothea, Halifax, Whig, March 1, 1831, 3
Winston, Edmund, ————, Enquirer, Sept. 8, 1818, 3
Winston, George, Richmond, Whig, Feb. 28, 1826, 3
Winston, Henry L., Louisa, Whig, Sept. 2, 1836, 2
Winston, Henry R., Hanover, Whig, Feb. 14, 1830, 3
Winston, Gen. Horatio G., ————, Whig, Dec. 2, 1836, 1
Winston, Mrs. Jane, Hanover, Whig, March 6, 1835, 1
Winston, Mrs. Louisa B., Hanover, Enquirer, Dec. 13, 1823, 3
-Winston, Mary, Richmond, Enquirer, Dec. 17, 1811, 3
Winston, Mrs. Nancy C., Hanover, Enquirer, June 1, 1816, 3
Winston, Sarah Elizabeth, Hanover, Enquirer, Nov. 14, 1823, 3
Winston, William, Amelia, Enquirer, April 19, 1805, 3
Wise, Ann E., Accomac, Whig, May 23, 1837, 1
Wiseman, William, Richmond, Enquirer, Aug. 9, 1805, 3
Wolfe, Benjamin, Richmond, Enquirer, Feb. 4, 1817, 3
Wolfe, Mrs. Sophia, Richmond, Enquirer, Nov. 10, 1820, 3
Wood, George, Jr., Lunenburg, Enquirer, Oct. 19, 1824, 3
Wood, Gen. James, near Richmond, Enquirer, June 29, 1813, 3
Wood, James, Richmond, Enquirer, June 18, 1813, 3
Wood, Jane, Albemarle, Enquirer, Nov. 9, 1810, 3
Wood, Mrs. Jean, Richmond, Enquirer, March 7, 11, 1823, 3
Wood, John, Richmond, Enquirer, May 17, 1822, 3
Wood, Mrs. Mary, Chesterfield, Enquirer, Jan. 6, 1824, 3
Wood, Mrs. Mercy, Granville, Enquirer, Aug. 7, 1827, 3
Wood, Rige W., Albemarle, Whig, April 30, 1833, 2
Wood, Mrs. Sarah O., Fluvanna, Whig, March 24, 1836, 3
Woodcock, Mrs. Isabella, Richmond, Whig, Sept. 12, 1831, 3
Woodfin, Ann Price, Richmond, Whig, Jan. 9, 1838, 4
Woodfin, Frances Ann, Richmond, Whig, Feb. 16, 1838, 4
Woodford, Mrs. Sarah C., Caroline, Enquirer, April 27, 1827, 3
Wooding, George W., Pittsylvania, Whig, Aug. 5, 1836, 1
Woods, Andrew, Jefferson, Whig, Nov. 28, 1837, 2
Woods, Mikiel, Lexington, Whig, July 18, 1826, 3
Woods, Robert H., Albemarle, Whig, Jan. 16, 1838, 1
Woodson, Mrs. Ann S., Buckingham, Enquirer, March 14, 1826, 3
Woodson, Col. Charles, Prince Edward, Whig, March 6, 1838, 2
Woodson, Charles L., Powhatan, Enquirer, Oct. 24, 1826, 3
Woodson, Maj. Frederick, Powhatan, Enquirer, Aug. 1, 1817, 3
Woodson, Frederick A., Cumberland, Enquirer, Nov. 28, 1817, 3
Woodson, John, Cumberland, Enquirer, Oct. 5, 1821, 3
Woodson, John, Lexington, Whig, Jan. 21, 1831, 3
Woodson, John P., Goochland, Enquirer, Aug. 16, 1815, 3
Woodson, Maj. Joseph, Goochland, Enquirer, Feb. 8, 1810, 3
Woodson, Mrs. Linton G., Powhatan, Enquirer, Oct. 24, 1826, 3
Woodson, Mathew, Richmond, Enquirer, July 15, 1828, 3; Whig, July 19, 1828, 3

Woodson, Robert H., Goochland, Enquirer, March 18, 1806, 3
Woodson, Capt. Samuel, Richmond, Enquirer, May 25, 1810, 3
Woodville, Mary S., Fincastle, Whig, June 21, 1836, 4
Woodward, Mrs. Lettice, Middlesex, Enquirer, Feb. 23, 1828, 3
Woody, Adeline M., Richmond, Whig, Oct. 24, 1834, 1
Woody, Elouisa Royall, Richmond, Whig, Nov. 24, 1835, 4
Woody, Mrs. Henry T., Chesterfield, Enquirer, Dec. 3, 1812, 3
Woody, Mrs. Mary, Richmond, Whig, Feb. 9, 1831, 3
Wooldridge, Dr. Beverly H., Chesterfield, Whig, Nov. 21, 1834, 1
Wooldridge, Dr. John, Chesterfield, Whig, Sept. 21, 1832, 3
Wooldridge, Granison B., Chesterfield, Whig, Jan. 12, 1836, 3
Wooldridge, Maj. Spencer, Chesterfield, Whig, Sept. 12, 1837, 4
Woolfolk, Elliott, [formerly of Virginia], Enquirer, Jan. 23, 1821, 3
Woolfolk, John G., Caroline, Enquirer, April 23, 1819, 3
Woolfolk, Richard, Caroline, Enquirer, May 30, 1820, 3
Word, Granville L., Richmond, Whig, Aug. 26, 1834, 1
Wormley, Ralph, Middlesex, Enquirer, March 11, 1815, 3
Worrall, Dr. James, Richmond, Enquirer, April 12, 1825, 3
Worsham, Mrs. Elizabeth, Prince Edward, Enquirer, Feb. 22, 1827, 3
Worsham, Capt. Wm., Prince Edward, Whig, Sept. 20, 1836, 4
Wortham, Mrs. Sarah Woolfolk, Amherst, Enquirer, March 22, 1822, 3
Wragg, Lieut. Joseph, Norfolk, Whig, April 22, 1825, 3
Wren, Elizabeth, Richmond, Enquirer, Nov. 1, 1811, 3
Wren, John, Richmond, Whig, Aug. 14, 1838, 4
Wren, Mrs. Theodicia, Richmond, Whig, Sept. 13, 1828, 3
Wrenn, Maj. Charles, Isle of Wight, Whig, April 21, 1837, 2
Wright, Gustavus W. T., Queen Anne, Enquirer, March 11, 1823, 3
Wright, Mrs. Mary, Buckingham, Enquirer, Dec. 9, 1815, 3
Wright, Mrs. Mary D., Essex, Enquirer, Oct. 3, 1823, 3
Wyatt, James, Gloucester, Whig, Oct. 8, 1824, 3
Wyatt, John W., Richmond, Enquirer, May 30, 1809, 3
Wyatt, Joseph M., Caroline, Enquirer, Aug. 12, 1823, 3
Wydown, Rev. Samuel, Fredericksburg, Enquirer, March 4, 1823, 3
Wynn, Robert, Dinwiddie, Whig, Dec. 21, 1824, 3; Enquirer, Dec. 21, 1824, 3
Wyse, Maria Louisa, Richmond, Whig, Sept. 22, 1831, 2
Wythe, George, ————, Enquirer, June 10, 1806, 3

Y.

Yancey, Mrs. Ann, Buckingham, Enquirer, Dec. 13, 1814, 3
Yancey, Mrs. Anne, Yanceyville, Enquirer, March 28, 1806, 3
Yancey, David, Louisa, Enquirer, Jan. 30, 1808, 3
Yarbrough, Elisha, Sr., Hanover, Whig, Jan. 2, 1835, 3
Yateman, Thomas R., Mathews, Whig, Sept. 28, 1832, 1
Yates, William, Brunswick, Enquirer, Sept. 17, 1822, 3
Yeatman, Thomas Robinson, Gloucester, Whig, May 20, 1836, 3
Yeatman, Thomas Y., Gloucester, Whig, May 17, 1836, 1

Young, Mrs. Eleanor F., Prince George, Whig, Nov. 29, 1831, 3
Young, Capt. Henry, near Tappahannock, Enquirer, Dec. 16, 1825, 3
Young, Mrs. Jane, Caroline, Whig, Nov. 24, 1835, 4
Younghusband, Sally Ann, Henrico, Whig, Nov. 1, 1828, 3